Village ON THE HILL

the story of Colehill in Dorset

George Sadler

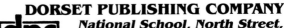
DORSET PUBLISHING COMPANY
*National School, North Street,
Wincanton, Somerset BA9 9AT*

Publishing details. First published 1992. Copyright George Sadler © 1992. All rights reserved. No part of this publication may be reproduced in any form or by any means, electronic, computerised, mechanical, photocopying, recording or otherwise, without prior permission in writing from the author.

Printing credits. Typesetting input by Reg Ward at Holwell, Dorset, and output by Wordstream Limited, St. Aldhelm's Road, Poole. Printed by The Fairwood Press, Westbury, Wilts. (telephone 0373 822044).

Distribution. Orders by post serviced by Dorset Publishing Company from the Wincanton Press, National School, North Street, Wincanton, Somerset BA9 9AT (telephone 0963 32583). Local distribution, to shops in the Dorset area, being undertaken for Dorset Publishing Company by Maurice Hann from 36 Langdon Road, Parkstone, Poole, Dorset BH14 9EH (telephone 0202 738248).

International standard book number. ISBN 0 948699 34 5

Contents

STREET MAP: COLEHILL AREA, 1950   4—5
ORDNANCE SURVEY MAP, 1885   6—7
Map of THE HANHAM ESTATE   8—9
ACKNOWLEDGEMENTS   11
Introduction   THE CHANGING FACE   13
1   IN THE BEGINNING   19
2   THE GREAT ESTATES   24
3   HOLLOW WAYS AND HIGHWAYS   34
4   THE VILLAGE TAKES SHAPE   46
5   THE PARISH IS CREATED   68
6   INTO THE TWENTIETH CENTURY   77
7   THE GREAT WAR AND THE TWENTIES   93
8   THE THIRTIES AND THE SECOND WORLD WAR   125
9   MODERN TIMES   142

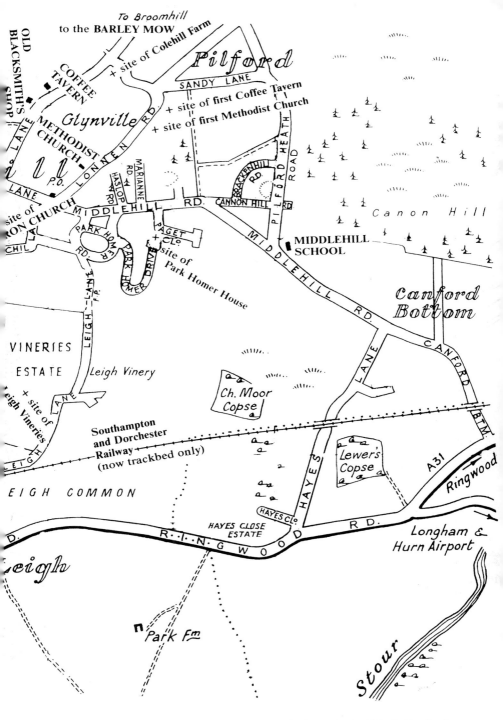

MID-TWENTIETH CENTURY STREET-MAP of Colehill, Pilford, Canford Bottom, Leigh and the central part of Wimborne.

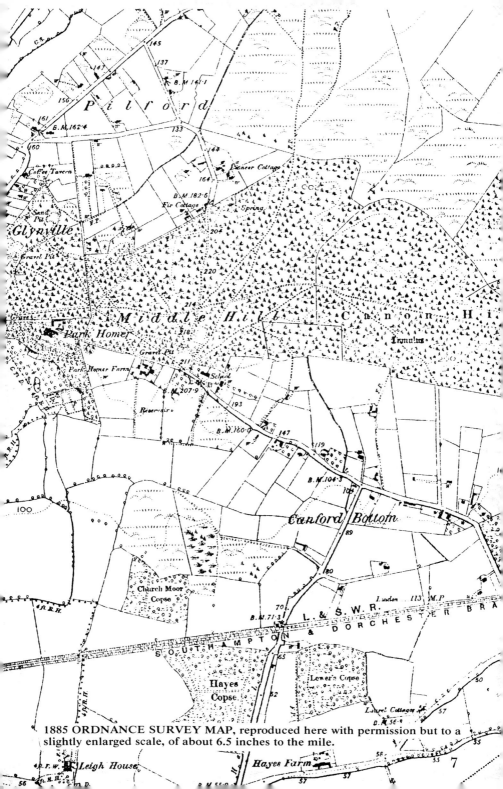

1885 ORDNANCE SURVEY MAP, reproduced here with permission but to a slightly enlarged scale, of about 6.5 inches to the mile.

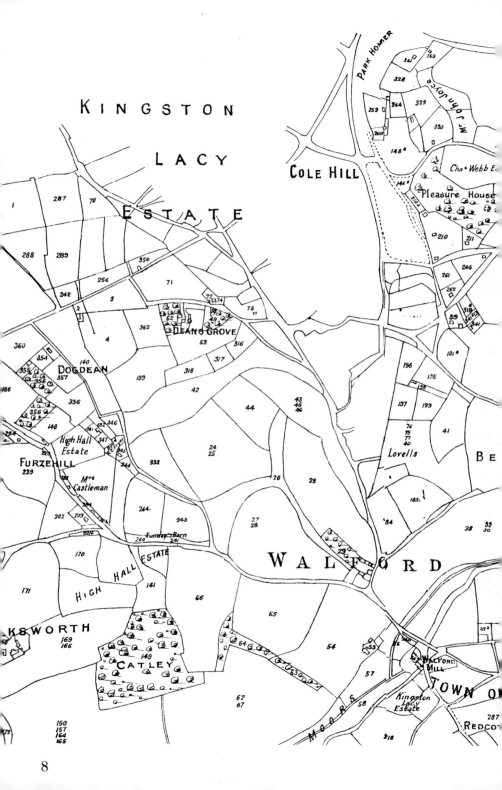

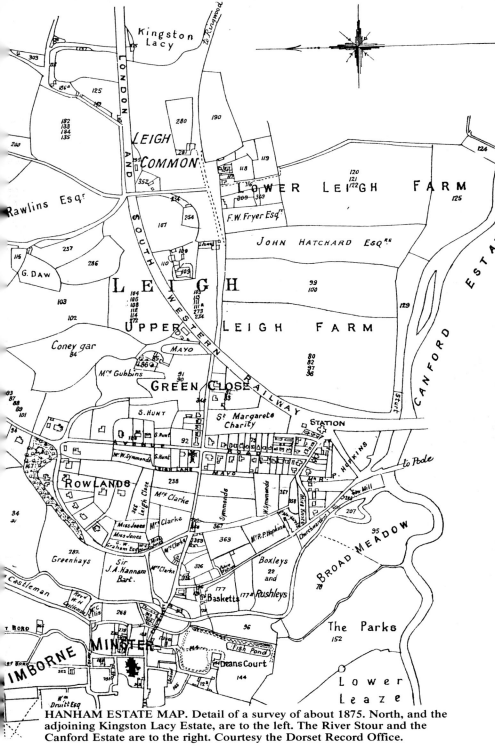

HANHAM ESTATE MAP. Detail of a survey of about 1875. North, and the adjoining Kingston Lacy Estate, are to the left. The River Stour and the Canford Estate are to the right. Courtesy the Dorset Record Office.

Acknowledgements

No history of this nature could be put together without the assistance of a great many people, to whom I am very much indebted. Some have gone to considerable trouble in unearthing ancient documents, maps and photographs. I would like to place on record my appreciation to everyone who has helped me.

My thanks go, first, to my wife and family, especially for their encouragement. Dorene spent long hours with me going through the archives at Dorchester. Paul, many years ago, when I started my researches, patiently transcribed tape recorded notes into a more accessible form; more recently, he has initiated me into the mysteries of the word processor, and has patiently "held my hand" when gremlins got into the works. And John has procured for me some important works of reference.

Secondly, I would like to thank, for their invaluable assistance, Sarah Bridges and her colleagues at the Dorset Record Office; Stephen Price, Kate Osborne and their helpers, particularly Dawn Nicolls and Gwen O'Brien, at the Priest's House Museum; and the staff at the Poole Reference Library.

Thirdly, I would like to record my gratitude to the following individuals: Mrs Eileen Allen, Ted Baldwin, Edgar Benham, Mrs Frances Burden, Mrs Phoebe Burden, Miss Selina Bush, Mrs Olive Butler, Miss Lily Christopher, Mrs Gladys Cole, Sidney and Doreen Cole, Mr and Mrs Dennis Curran, John Dacombe, Mrs Olive Damen, Mrs Gillian Fox, Miss Mildred Gillett, Rev John Goodall, Lt.-Col George Gray, A. Gwynne, Ralph Habgood, Miss Margaret Hewett, Merrick Jackson, Maurice Jenkins, Mrs Audrey Jupe, Rev David Le Seelleur, Mrs Barbara Marriott, Frank Middleton, Major William Naesmythe of

OPPOSITE
PARISH CHURCH AND ROAD SIGNS, the former a unique European implant on the Dorset scene by architect William Douglas Caroe in 1893, and the latter surviving from the 1930s generation of sign-posts that were a contribution to charms of a more leisured countryside. Photographed by Rodney Legg in 1991.

Posso, Mrs Grace Nisbet, Robin Noscoe, John Pantlin, David Parker, Richard Pink, Derek and Margaret Pope, Harold Pressley, Mrs D.K. Priddle, Mrs Muriel Rowe, Mrs Rene Sawtell, Dick Selby, Jim Selby, Miss Betty Shiner, Miss Irene Smart, David Smith, Ivor Thomas, Mrs Kathleen Thorner, Stanley and Margaret Walker, Col. P. Wavish, Mrs Bill Webster, Jim Welch, Reg West, Peter and Ruth White, Mrs Vera Williams and Ian Willis.

Time takes its inexorable toll, and all too many of those who have helped me in my researches over the years have, alas, since died. These I remember with much gratitude: David Bryant, David Cobb, Walter Cole, Henry Habgood, Claude Hanbury-Tracy-Domville, Miss Elizabeth Osman, Frank Peckham, Charlie Sawtell, Mrs Clara Smart, George Watson and Garney Williams.

WESTERN END OF COLEHILL, seen from the air in the 1950s. Looking south-east, up Beaucroft Road, with Wimborne Road crossing the picture from the left to bottom centre. It then turns to the right, where the cricket pitch is visible, with the pavilion in the lower right-hand corner. Greenhill Road runs off to the left, at the bottom left-hand edge of the picture.

Introduction

THE CHANGING FACE

"In 1865, when Colonel Leopold Paget, Royal Artillery, came to live at Park Homer, he found a rather wild and lawless population scattered over the heath country..."

Reading these words, written by the Colonel's widow in a fine copperplate, in a beautiful vellum book, sparked off, in a very real sense, this work; or, perhaps more accurately, added some fuel to the spark. I became increasingly interested in tracing the story of these "wild and lawless" people.

The idea of setting down the history of Colehill had originated a little while earlier. I moved to Colehill with my family early in 1963 (at which time, to put the record straight, I found the population to be eminently respectable and law-abiding) and we made our home in one of the bungalows on the newly-developed Vineries housing estate. Between the wars, there had been some new building in the form of council houses and privately-owned bungalows in Middlehill Road, but these, and the erection of more council houses at Marshfield and New Merrifield after the 1939-45 war, had not basically altered the character of the village. The bulk of the residents were genuinely local people.

And then came the Vineries Estate, and the invasion of Colehill by a horde of foreigners. The blight had set in. But even this made little impression on Colehill itself as a good proportion of the newcomers became orientated to Wimborne rather than to the village. The dependence of modern man (and woman) on the motor car was in large measure responsible for this, coupled with the peculiarity of the local geography, which resulted in its being as quick to travel to Wimborne by car as to drive to the centre of Colehill village. This still remains the case now, nearly 30 years later.

I was fortunate, therefore, in coming to live in Colehill when I did, and while it was relatively unspoiled, to be able to get to know the village and to feel that I really "belonged" to it.

In due course, all the heathland north of Middlehill Road between Cannon Hill and Lonnen Road disappeared under bricks and mortar, in what we now call the "Marshbirds Estate" (or "The Bird Sanctuary"). The land to the east of Hayes Lane, previously occupied only by Fox Farm and one or two nurseries, became another housing estate; and then the land to the west of Hayes Lane was built upon. And Wimborne marches on across the fields from the south-west, and the houses advance, too, from the south-east, and up the tree-clad slopes of Cannon Hill, almost to the crest.

The village school expanded, to accommodate the vast new population of children; new classrooms were built on what was once an extensive playing field, ending in an attractive little grove of trees – these, too, have been encroached upon with the erection, first, of the local Public Library, and then, more recently, the Village Memorial Hall. Not only has the Middlehill School, the original village school, multiplied its numbers, but no fewer than four completely new schools have been built in the village, while the arrival of Dumpton at Deans Grove has brought the total to six. Two of the new schools were erected in the woodland between St Michael's Church and the Wimborne road; and at the start and close of the school day, during term-time, the volume of traffic at the intersections, at the Church, the War Memorial and the Post Office, puts one rather in mind of Piccadilly Circus.

In 28 years, I, a newcomer myself, have seen the face of Colehill change completely. A good enough reason, it might be argued, for my setting down my memories of the place as I found it. But a second, more potent, reason for writing this story now presented itself. Whereas the population in the newly developed districts consisted largely of young married couples and their offspring, a high percentage of the "real" village people were elderly.

These good folk would remember a Colehill I never knew, before the war of 1939-45. Some of them, indeed, might remember the village in an even more spacious and leisurely age, before the Great War of 1914-18. However, they would not always be with us to tell their tales, and their memories would pass on with them, and so be lost for ever to posterity. These thoughts brought an element of urgency to my task and I decided, without more ado, to collect all available material for this history of Colehill.

I set to work to discover who were the oldest inhabitants and to contact those whose memories were least dimmed by the passing years. And these men and women, without a single exception so far as I can recall, dipped freely into their memories, and sometimes their photograph albums also, for my benefit. I hope and believe that they enjoyed doing so; I know that, for my part, I derived immense pleasure from these meetings which helped to piece together the story of old Colehill. High and humble, residents of the "Big Houses" and those of cottages alike, were unfailingly courteous, interested in my work (which was, of course, a great encouragement) and helpful where they could be. Younger people, too, helped me in my researches; they had inherited ancient photographs, or had remembered stories of the past handed on from parents, aunts and uncles.

These people have been the custodians of the history of Colehill – to them all, I am very grateful, and to them all, I dedicate this book.

And so I learned to find my way along thoroughfares with half-forgotten names, up Glyn's Hill and Sweetapple Lane, down The Slop to Brick Hill, or down past the Coffee Tavern to Patey's, as I walked, in search of history, on Colehill.

I learned also the correct pronunciation of the name – Col-hill – the "o" is short, not long. One did not live, I gathered, *in* Colehill, one lived *on Col-hill*, or more simply, on the Hill. There has been much speculation on the derivation of the name, and there is no definitive explanation.

However, one can make a reasonably educated guess. There were certainly never any coal mines in the area.

However, one theory which has been suggested, that charcoal may well have been produced in this "heavily wooded area" once upon a time, and that this was the origin of the name, is supported by an entry in the 1881 Census, which records a charcoal manufacturer named Charles Long living in the district. On the other hand, it must be remembered that most of the "heavy woodland" which crowned the hill in the last hundred years or so consisted of pine trees, of comparatively recent growth. In the days when charcoal was produced in any quantity, the whole of the top of the hill would have been open heath country. One is inclined, therefore, to dismiss any connection with coal.

Possibly, Col (or Cole, or some other variant) was the name of a Saxon settler. Yet another theory is that "col" or "coll" is an old Dorset word meaning hazel, and certainly the Celtic "cole" had that meaning; and that Colehill was the hill on which hazels grew, just as the proliferation of other shrubs gave Broomhill and Furzehill their names. Whether there was an abundance of hazel trees on Colehill at one time is something we are unlikely to discover.

However, one comes back to the correct pronunciation and old spelling – *Col*-hill – together with the physical configuration of the place, in a search for another answer. The "Hill" element of the name is self-explanatory, and my dictionary informs me that "Col" is derived from the Latin word "collum", meaning neck. And this appears to me to be the most logical derivation – "neck" conjoined to "hill" – Col-hill – not only accounts for the pronunciation, but also exactly describes the place: a neck-shaped hill, some two and a half miles in length, and at no point more than three-quarters of a mile wide. Look south from, say, Broomhill, or northwards from Canford Magna, and the distinctive "shape" of Col-hill is quite apparent.

Walk the two and a half miles along the "spine" of Colehill, from the top of St John's Hill, up Rowlands Hill, along Wimborne Road and Middlehill Road and then along the bridleway to the Bronze Age round barrows on Cannon Hill, and you can still enjoy the distant views at intervals along the way, on either side. To the left you can see, on a fine day, as far as Cranborne Chase; on the right, the view extends across the Stour Valley to Bournemouth, and beyond, to the Isle of Wight. In the early years of this century, before the trees and the houses grew in such profusion, you would have had an unimpeded view for the whole of the journey.

Whether one accepts the Celtic, Latin or Saxon origins of the name, the pronunciation of Colehill has survived, but the spelling has changed over the years. Lady Greathed, who lived at Uddens House, mentions Col Hill – two words – in her diary for February 1880, but the "e" had crept in much earlier, and there are references to Col*e*hill dating as far back as 1535.

In gathering material for this story, I have used a somewhat arbitrary definition of what constitutes the village of Colehill today. The Civil Parish includes within its boundaries districts which seem to have no affinity with the village – the area south of the old railway line, for example, or, to the west, hamlets such as Clapgate and Furzehill. The boundaries of the Ecclesiastical Parish conform much better to one's general idea of the extent of the village. But in the end, I have fallen back on my derivation of the name Colehill, the neck-shaped hill, and identify the village as the area bounded by the 150-feet contour. This story, then, tells of the past of this elongated piece of land, and of small areas to the north and south which are clearly part of the village.

I have, of course, in choosing these boundaries, strayed across the frontiers of the neighbouring Ecclesiastical Parishes of Hampreston, Holt and Wimborne Minster. Inevitably, for a village in such close proximity to Wimborne, the threads of the tale are inextricably interwoven with those of the town; and other places "off the map", so to speak, are also involved, particularly bearing in mind that large parts of the district were, and indeed, to a lesser extent, still are, owned by the Kingston Lacy and Uddens Estates.

History books can sometimes make dull reading. They never should. I have tried, as well as I can, to bring the history to life, painting, I hope, a vivid picture, with recorded fact and verbal anecdote, eked out with reasonable probabilities and a little imagination. I am reminded by another historian, John Haime, one-time resident of Colehill, in a lively account of his ancestors called *The Haimes – a Dorset Family*, of the words of Ezekiel in the valley of bones:

"Lo, they were very dry. And he said unto me, Son of man, can these bones live? ... There was a noise, and behold a shaking, and the bones came together, bone to his bone. And when I beheld, lo, the sinews and the flesh came up upon them and the skin covered them above ... And the breath came into them, and they lived."

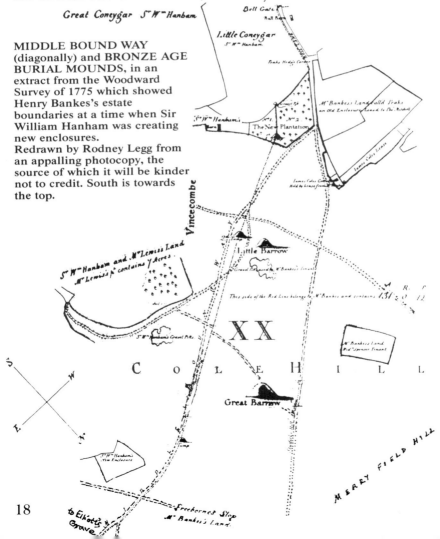

MIDDLE BOUND WAY (diagonally) and BRONZE AGE BURIAL MOUNDS, in an extract from the Woodward Survey of 1775 which showed Henry Bankes's estate boundaries at a time when Sir William Hanham was creating new enclosures.
Redrawn by Rodney Legg from an appalling photocopy, the source of which it will be kinder not to credit. South is towards the top.

Chapter 1

IN THE BEGINNING

How far back can we dip into history, before certainty fades into mere speculation? Three, four, perhaps five millenia, for the experts tell us that Mesolithic Man lived in this district before the New Stone Age, and that Neolithic Man followed him. We can certainly trace the story of Colehill back, dimly, a matter of thirty-six or thirty-seven centuries (which is probably a longer history than even Wimborne can claim).

There can be no doubt that this hilly area was populated in the Early Bronze Age. We have evidence of this in the round barrows at the eastern end of the trackway along the "spine" of Cannon Hill, and those on what used to be known as "Jenny (or Ginny) Down" behind what is now St Michael's School. These ancient burial grounds still remain, from about 2,000 years before Christ, while so much that has come since has been obliterated. We have scant knowledge of the people who settled on the heath all those years ago, but may assume that they lived a nomadic existence, moving on from place to place, and taking their herds of cattle with them.

Skipping a mere 1,200 years or so, we come to the dawn of the Iron Age. Round about the year 450 BC, one can visualise the then residents of Colehill gazing down one morning from a tree-less Cannon Hill, or a bungalow-less Middle Hill, to see a flotilla of ships wending its way up the River Stour from the English Channel. The Celts were invading our shores, bringing with them, from France, their crude iron implements. They established their hill-forts beside the Stour at Hod Hill and Hambledon Hill, upstream of modern Blandford, and nearer at hand, at Buzbury Rings and Badbury Rings. We have no positive evidence, but it seems inconceivable that this chain of defences guarding the vital trade route up the river, which was continued with Dudsbury, downstream, and Hengistbury, overlooking Christchurch Harbour, should not also have included Colehill. We can, at least, be sure that the invaders soon settled in the area, no doubt enjoying, as we latter-day invaders also enjoy, the pleasant mild climate.

Parallel with the river, the Celts made a track (or perhaps improved on an existing one) to link their chain of hill-forts and to victual their garrisons and the settlements. In his book, *The Old Roads of Dorset*, Ronald Good suggested that the track ran from Christchurch Harbour, by way of St Catherine's Hill, across what is now the aerodrome at Hurn, over Parley Common (at Gibbet Firs) to Dudsbury, then on to Stapehill, Cannon Hill, Colehill, Wimborne, Badbury and Buzbury. Colehill was thus on the map, and moreover, on an important trade route. A considerable part of this track survives to the present day, particularly in Colehill, much of it carrying a substantial motor traffic. The bridle-track along the "spine" of Cannon Hill, continuing along Middlehill Road to the Post Office, and Wimborne Road as far as the Cricket Ground, is, in all probability, on the very line of this original route, dating from four centuries or so before the Romans came.

Professor Good gave it as his opinion that a further track branched off at the eastern end of Cannon Hill, near the round barrows, running to the north. This branch might have led to Bokerly Down, and probably extended in a southerly direction, beyond Cannon Hill, to the river at Canford, and then on to Barrow Hill at Corfe Mullen, to link up with a further track from Hengistbury Head. Colehill, then, would not only have appeared on an Iron Age map of Dorset, standing on a trade route, but would have been the site of an important crossroads, at Cannon Hill.

As we move on towards the end of the Iron Age era, the hill-forts were enlarged, and we can, perhaps, picture our tracks carrying a considerable volume of traffic, and the likelihood of a fair-sized Celtic community living on Colehill.

In studying the early trackways which led to or through Colehill, one must bear in mind the close proximity of the River Stour, and consider to what extent, as distinct from being a natural route in itself, it constituted a barrier to transport. It was many hundreds of years before the building of any bridges, of course, and there were only two practical places where the Stour could be forded in the district. One of these was very close to where the Julians Bridge now spans the river at Wimborne. The other, immediately below Colehill, gave Canford part of its name. The situation of the ford will have been largely instrumental in determining the line of the trade routes. Where these converged or crossed, settlements became established and flourished. By the same token, as the river was bridged, so Colehill declined. Traffic from the south, crossing the Stour by Canford Bridge, would find its way through Wimborne instead.

The Belgic invasion, followed by the conquest of the hill-forts, was quickly succeeded by the influx of a further foreign host – the might of Rome. With the arrival of the Romans, there was a much greater development of the low-lying parts of the countryside. We can be sure that the Romans soon controlled the hill-forts, in the early years of the first century AD, and much evidence of the Roman occupation still survives in the locality: the site of a Roman villa a mile or two away, for example, and the clearly defined arrow-straight roads radiating like the spokes of a wheel from the important road junction and camp that Badbury Rings had become.

As it happened, none of these roads passed directly through Colehill. But at the only point where the road to Hamworthy, on Poole Harbour, deviated from the straight, near its crossing of the Stour, a branch turned off to the east, through Wimborne, and on to Winchester. Although not dead straight in the normal fashion of the Roman engineers, it was reasonably direct. Leigh Road, – the old A31 trunk road – eastwards out of Wimborne, is its modern counterpart and indeed, follows very close to the line of that original road, as it keeps to the low ground, north of the river, and running along below Colehill. This route dates from about 180 AD and has thus been in use more or less continuously for about 1,800 years.

More troubled times lay ahead, with raids by the Saxons,

and the decline and fall of the power of Rome. Peaceful Saxon settlers came up the Stour from Christchurch, before the main Saxon invasion. No doubt they settled on the drier, higher ground overlooking the river: one cannot be sure, of course, but may conjecture that some of these early Saxons made their home on Colehill.

Within little more than a hundred years, the Saxons had conquered and settled the greater part of the country. Hard on their heels came St Augustine and the other early missionaries who converted the English to Christianity. Wimborne – or Wimburnia – had become established in Roman times and it evidently prospered, becoming an ecclesiastical centre of some considerable importance. Ine, King of Wessex, gave land in the town to his sister, Cuthburga, in 705 for the establishment of a monastery for nuns as well as monks.

The siting of the monastery, with royal sponsorship, clearly established the pre-eminence of Wimborne over the whole neighbourhood down the years. In the centuries that followed, with the development of culture, learning and scholarship, the literate classes, stemming without exception from the religious foundation, left behind them records and accounts of their town. Wimborne therefore thrived and became an important centre for the whole of the surrounding district, while Colehill, up there on the heath, remained shrouded in the mists of antiquity for many more centuries. Wimborne was already the mother church of Hampreston and Holt, and so the whole of what eventually became the Ecclesiastical Parish of Colehill came under the jurisdiction of Wimborne. Even today, Colehill is part of the Wimborne Rural Deanery; and furthermore, the Governors of Wimborne Minster remain the patrons of the Parish of Colehill, and so have the living within their gift.

The raids by the Vikings were followed by the first Danish conquest. Guthrum might well have led his Danes over Colehill on his way from the north through Wimborne to Wareham in 876.

No specific mention, though, is made of Colehill during

the Saxon era, but both Uddens, on the eastern fringes, and Leigh, to the south, and still giving its name to the Common and two or three roads, are recorded. Wimborne was part of the "Tything" of Leigh. The modern pronunciation of Leigh makes it rhyme with 'sky", but the original pronunciation, still used by many older villagers, was "Lee". The change seems to have come in Victorian times when, perhaps, the new version sounded superior to the newly arrived aristocracy.

A charter of 958 makes a reference to Uddingc – the modern Uddens – named after a Saxon leader, Udda, who settled there. This is of much interest in view of the considerable impact made on the eastern part of Colehill much later by the Uddens Estate. It is more than possible that Udda himself walked up Cannon Hill over a thousand years ago and laid claim to a tract of the heathland.

DONKEY LANE, in the trees bottom left, and St Audrey's and Wingreen in Greenhill Close, seen from the air, from the north-west, in the 1950s. The village cricket pitch is visible in the top right-hand corner.

Chapter 2

THE GREAT ESTATES

Wimborne, we have seen, was already, by the time of the Norman Conquest, a town of some considerable importance, certainly in ecclesiastical terms, and since the religious community virtually constituted the literate class of the population, one can safely assume that Wimborne also became a centre of scholarship as well as the hub of the commercial life of the district.

Nothing seems to have been recorded of Colehill, however, for another three hundred years, although there is a record, in 1066, of a track passing to the north-west, below the hill, along the line of the roads that we know today as Burts Hill and Long Lane, running from Wimborne up towards Verwood. One can guess, perhaps, at a scattering of humble dwellings up on the heath.

Leigh and Uddens continue to be mentioned in various documents, but the first specific mention of Colehill itself does not appear before the year 1341, when it was spelt Colhulle. In 1365, it was known as Cokeshull (which may, perhaps, be regarded as "fuel" for the "charcoal" theory on the derivation of the place-name).

A source known as the "Valor Ecclesiasticus", a valuation of ecclesiastical property, ordered by the Crown on the eve of the Dissolution of the Monasteries, in 1535, included an entry for "Colehill" – note the modern spelling – "within the rural Deanery of Pimperne".

A legacy of 1561 created a charity, "Boxley's Gift", which has directly benefitted the Church of St Michael at Colehill, although it concerned land at Rowlands, a meadow called Rushley, which hardly lies within the scope of this story. Thomas Boxley left this land to John Welstead and Christopher Mackam and their successors, half the profits to go to the poor and half to such "Good and Godly workes" as the trustees should think fit. 360 years later, the "Gift" contributed £25 to the cost of retiling the roof of Colehill Church tower.

Saxton's map of Dorsetshire fails to show Colehill, or any variation of the name, in 1575, but a deed dated 1584 or 1585 records "A demise of lands and tenements by Theodore Sadler, gent., of London, to Thomas Hanam, Esq., of Wimborne Minster, among them "a house at Collehill in the tenure of Cyrile Hardinge and an acre of land at Collehill in the tenure of Thomas Willis". (This sixteenth century owner of property on Colehill, incidentally, is not related, so far as can be traced, to the author). Thomas Hanam was a member of the Hanham family, of Deans Court, Wimborne, who were substantial land owners in the district, and who are happily still with us today.

References in legal documents such as these constitute virtually the only record of Colehill down the years. A further example is the will of Thomas Oates, dated March 1637. Among his bequests is that of his "ground and tythes of Colehill".

The district is mentioned elsewhere in the Wimborne Minster archives. In 1637, there is a record of a Deed on a cottage at "Uddings", and in the same year, a "roughlease" tenement called "Gyddielake"; and in 1654, of a "messuage and three closes near Colehill on south and east of commons". A cottage "lately burnt down at Colehill" is recorded in 1708.

Other references occur in the records of the meetings of the Court Leet for the Manors of Wimborne Deanery and Leigh. George Hassey was "presented" in April 1774 "for inclosing several lanes belonging to Leigh Common. Same to be thrown open in three months under penalty of £10". Hassey apparently failed to comply for several years and the penalty was progressively increased. At the Court in 1775, John Tory, junior, "took delivery of a Toft and Close called am Howe lying at Colehill containing three acres in the tenure of Roger Tilsed". Tilsed held the property "according to the custom of the Manor of Wimborne Deanery by virtue of a copy of a Court Roll dated 29th September 1698" for a yearly rent of two shillings. Tory, as sole purchaser, gave the Lord (Sir William Hanham, Bart.) a "fine" of £15. Another record dating from 1775 is of

25

"one Parrock or Parcell of Ground on which a tenement or cottage formerly stood containing half an acre and a close of arable land lying in Leigh field near a close called Rowlands containing three acres, in the tenure of Mary Harvey". Mary was the widow of James Harvey and the property reverted to Richard Combes. The land at "am Howe" is mentioned again five years later. Leigh Common is mentioned in the Court proceedings for 1780. Cattle were apparently being grazed on the Common by those with no rights. Instructions were given to Thomas Green, the Hayward of Leigh, to impound these animals, a fine of two shillings and sixpence being imposed for each animal. One shilling of this would go to a fund for draining the Common and the rest to the Hayward "for his trouble".

But we have rather over-run our story. So much of the history of Colehill is bound up with the fortunes of the great estates of the landed gentry, particularly those of the Bankes, Hanham and Greathed families, who owned the vast majority of the land in the district. The most important of these was the estate based on the manor house some four miles away, on the other side of Wimborne, at Kingston Lacy.

The Manor of Kingston Lacy was owned by the Crown in Norman times, but Henry I gave the property to the Earl of Millent, Robert de Beaumont, Count of Meulan, early in the twelfth century. A descendant of his granted the estate in 1229 to John de Lasey, who later became the Earl of Lincoln.

The Manor was divided into Tithings, one of which was the Tithing of Leigh, covering the district to the east of Wimborne, in the valley of the Stour, and north of the river, including the southern part of Colehill. The area further north, covering most of the present village, came within the Tithing of Thornhill.

The sub-manor of "Uddyng" was absorbed into the estate in 1313, but only for a short period. A fourteenth century map shows that Uddens had become, once again, autonomous, the boundary between the two estates conforming to that followed more than 500 years later, when the modern civil parishes were created, by the border between Colehill and Hampreston – prior to the amendment of 1913. This early record shows the vast extent of the Kingston Lacy domains, stretching from the River Stour, in the south, to almost as far north as Pentridge, and from Shapwick, in the west, to Three Legged Cross, in the east. The area had been halved 200 years later, and the northern boundary conformed to that of the modern parish of Holt. The Kingston Lacy Estate Survey of 1549 records: "... *their pertayneth too the said manor a hethe called Collehill cont by est 160 a.*" – so the surveyors estimated the extent of the heath at Colehill at 160 acres at that time. It is clear from a survey of 1590, nearly sixty years before the estate was purchased by Sir John Bankes, that the western half of Colehill lay within its boundaries. The eastern part of the hill lay within the confines of the Uddens Estate. The 1590 survey of "The Manor of Kingeston Lacie, Dorsetshire" has a record of the perambulation, or boundaries, of the estate. The boundary on the eastern side ran more or less northward from the River Stour, opposite "Canford Parke" (which we know nowadays as the grounds of Canford School).

It is by no means easy to trace the exact line of this ancient boundary on the modern map, the survey, brought up-to-date with a revision in 1775 – the Woodward Survey, referring to hedges and ditches and other features, some of which have no doubt disappeared under the influence of modern farming methods – to say nothing of new housing estates. The boundary crossed "the Highway which leadeth to Wimborne Westward", with the Uddens Estate to its east, and seems to have followed a somewhat zig-zag line roughly parallel to Leigh Lane, and there seems little doubt that some of these hedges and ditches still marking the boundary of the remains of the estate, now in the ownership of the National Trust, must be of great antiquity.

The boundary continued "following the same way which leadeth Northward towards the heath called Colehill". Reference is made hereabouts to "Sfursty Hayes" and "Pepping's Haye", the exact location of which cannot be traced, but it seems almost certain that these names are perpetuated in the district now known as Hayes, and the road running to the north from it, Hayes Lane.

The perambulation goes on up the hill "directly North thwarting the Heath to a dubble ditch and so to the end of the said ditch therehence directly Eastward over Parkesse Hill". The revision notes referring to the "dubble ditch" record that this is "Now visible, and is a deep dry ditch on the top of Colehill at Elliott's Grave". The site of Elliott's Grave was very close to the present junction of Middlehill Road and the eastern end of Park Homer Road and was marked, until recent times, by an ancient stone.

It is not known who Elliott was, but local folklore has it that he was hanged, and presumably buried, on this spot. An alternative theory, which has been suggested as the origin of the naming of this spot, is that the surveyor actually recorded "Elliott's Gravel Pit", and that a subsequent amputation by the cartographers turned the gravel pit into a grave. Another name for this location, recorded in old documents, is "Three Lords Lands", presumably the meeting place of the estates of the three great landowners at that time, Bankes, Hanham and Lord Arundel, or, perhaps, Lord Ashley.

Lord Arundel certainly owned land in the neighbourhood, and so too did Lord Ashley. A map, inherited by Claude Hanbury-Tracy-Domville, in the archives of the Uddens Estate, predating the Woodward Survey by one (or two) hundred years, of the "Mannor and Charme of Great and Little Uddens in the parish of Chawbury and County of Dorsett belonging to the Rt. Hon. the Lord Ashley" shows adjoining land as being owned partly by "Lord Arundell" and partly by "Sir Ralph Banks". The map is dated, but the second digit of the *year* is indecipherable, and could be either 1571 or 1671. "Chawbury" was the old spelling of Chalbury, and Uddens lay in a detached portion of that parish. In 1886, the detached part was amalgamated into what was then the parish of Wimborne.

There still stands, a few yards away from the site of

Elliott's Grave, one of the ancient boundary stones of the Bankes Estate, with the inscription, still legible, "Kingston Lacy 1775". The line of an old footpath appears to have been slightly moved over the years, so that the boundary stone now lies within the garden of a private house.

The revision goes on to say that "The end of this ditch is at the entrance of the swamp near Freeborne's slop". The accompanying map indicated this to be in the vicinity of Marshfield, whose name perpetuates the swampy nature of the neighbourhood, and the adjoining dip, slightly to the east of the church, in Smugglers Lane, is still known to the older generation as "The Slop". The revision describes "Parkesse Hill" as being "In Hampreston Heath, near Cannon Hill" and it goes on: "From this Hill, to Pilford Lane end, the boundary cannot be exactly traced ... there being so many dry ditches and old mounds near the hill."

The eighteenth century surveyor, referring to the heathland hereabouts, might well have been writing in the latter part of the twentieth century, as this remained barren heath country until the building of the "Marsh-birds" estate in the late 1960s. The revision clearly was not able to be too precise as to the boundary line, but it seems to have roughly conformed to the present-day limits of the Forestry Commission plantation at Cannon Hill. The whole of this plantation was owned at one time by the Uddens Estate, part of it subsequently being sold, and the rest of it leased, to the Forestry Commission.

While the rest of the district seems to have been enclosed from earlier times, the open common fields of the Kingston Lacy Estate were not enclosed until the Act of Parliament of 1786, for which the Woodward Survey provided the necessary information.

This survey indicates that the boundary between the Bankes and the Hanham Estates roughly followed a line from Dogdean running across country to the Horns Inn, then north-eastwards along Burts Hill and Long Lane. The land to the south and east of this belonged to Bankes, that to the north and west to Hanham, being part of the Manor of Wilksworth. The boundary on the south conformed to a trackway known as Middle Bound Way, approximately on the line now followed by Wimborne Road, as far as "The New Plantation", rather to the north of New Bell Gate, which stood in Bell Lane. The top section of the present-day St John's Hill roughly conforms to the old Bell Lane. The New Bell Gate was a short distance up the hill from its junction with the Old Road, which used to run to the west to a ford over the River Allen. The boundary would then have run westward as far as the Allen. The Bankes land lay to the west and north of this line, with the Hanham Estate, consisting of the Manors of Wimborne Minster, otherwise known as The Deanery, and Leigh, to the east and south. The "Old Bell Gate" was situated further down the hill along Bell Lane.

A legal document, also dating from 1775, the date of the Woodward Survey, traces the line of this boundary precisely, as it is in the form of an "Indenture", or agreement, between Henry Bankes and Sir William Hanham, over what seems to have been disputed territory on the top of Colehill. The argument seems to have gone on for a long while, and indeed, ended with Sir William being arraigned in the Court of the King's Bench. The disputed area amounted to about 26 acres of heath, of which two acres and 26 perches had been enclosed and planted with fir trees – the "New" Plantation – by Hanham.

This land, which would command a considerable price today, was of very little value in 1775. It is, indeed, described in the document as "Waste" – a legal term implying commonable untenanted manorial land – and the only things of value it contained at the time were gravel pits. In the end, the case was settled out of court, and damages amounting to one shilling were paid to Bankes. Further, Bankes, having established ownership of the land in dispute, agreed to lease the New Plantation to Hanham for a period of 200 years at an annual rent of one shilling.

The boundary is traced, from Bell Lane, near the meadows called Peaks and Coneygar (or Coniger), along Middle Bound Way, which is described as a "Green Way", to the double ditch near Elliott's Grave or the Three Lords

Lands. The Agreement gives alternative names for Bell Lane: Bells Lane or Colehill Lane (not to be confused with the modern Colehill Lane, which starts half a mile away, at its nearest point). Colehill Lane persisted as the name of this thoroughfare for at least another 86 years as the 1861 Census, clearly dealing with the Lewens Lane area of Wimborne, lists occupants with that address. Similarly confusing, we find, much more recently, Wimborne's Legg Lane shown on a map of 1875 as "Leigh Lane".

Queen Elizabeth I had granted the Manors of Wimborne Minster, Leigh and Wilksworth to Thomas and James Hanam in 1590.

Isaac Taylor's map of Dorset, dated about 1790, gives little detail of the area, locating such places as Coll Hill, Furzy Hill and Broomy Hill. "Uddins" is also marked and the map is, at least, commendably up-to-date in recording the name of the new tenant, Greathed, Esq. Nathaniel Gundry was the eighteenth century owner of the Uddens Estate, and leased it in that same year, 1790, to Edward Greathed, who subsequently purchased the freehold. The estate passed to a niece, Mary (née Greathed) and her husband, Edward Harris, a condition being that they assumed the family name "Greathed". A map of the Uddens Estate, dated about 1900, shows its western boundary to have run parallel to Lonnen Road, and to the west of it, to include Pilford Farm, then along Sandy Lane, and from there, southwards to Green Bottom and on to Church Moor Copse and the railway line. The triangle of land between Lonnen Road and Middlehill Road, beyond the Uddens Estate boundary, known as Glynville, belonged to the Gaunts Estate, owned by Sir Richard Glyn, who was related to the Greatheds by marriage.

Meanwhile, as we have noted, much of the land formerly within the confines of the Bankes Estate had been purchased by the Deanery Estate of Wimborne, in the ownership of the Hanham family. The Hanham Estate map, dated about 1875, shows the boundaries on Colehill much as they had been a hundred years before. The land to the south and west of a line roughly following Boundary

Drive, Wimborne Road and Leigh Lane lay within its area. Indeed, Boundary Drive could well have been so named from its forming part of the boundary between the Bankes and Hanham Estates, but it does, of course, nowadays form part of the boundary of the adjacent ground of the Colehill Cricket Club.

However, part of the estate had been sold off prior to 1875. John Joyce had become the owner of two fields to the east of Northleigh Lane, Charles Webb, the Wimborne maltster, owned land on the opposite side, and on this he built his Northleigh House, about 1862, and laid out his spacious grounds; and further down the hill, an area fifteen acres in extent, bounded by Beaucroft and Northleigh Lanes, was owned by Thomas Rawlins. Rawlins purchased this plot, which included a narrow strip of land on the western side of Beaucroft Lane, in 1867 from Camile Caillard and Alexander Copland, trustees of the will of Rev Sir James Hanham, who had died in 1849. Beaucroft House, its lodge and coachhouse were built in 1876.

The entire estate was purchased by Mrs Bernarda Lees in 1881, and she bought the remaining Hanham land in this part of Colehill, amounting to six acres, in 1885, from Phelips Brooke Hanham, who had inherited it from Sir James, and later, the Pleasure House Plantation. Except for the Northleigh property, Mrs Lees had become the owner of all the land bounded by Wimborne Road, Northleigh Lane and Beaucroft Lane, together with the narrow strip of land beyond Beaucroft Lane, to form the Beaucroft Estate.

Phelips Hanham also owned the land to the west of Beaucroft Lane, extending to St John's Hill. Following his death in 1917, this land was sold by auction at the Crown Hotel, Wimborne, by the Public Trustee. Tom Coakes, a greengrocer, purchased three acres of this land, adjoining the lower part of Beaucroft Lane, in 1919. The remaining area, between Northleigh Lane and Leigh Lane, had also been disposed of, to Charles Webb, and was later sold off by his Estate, some in small parcels of land, but much of it contained in pasture belonging to Joseph Stevenson, and the land, further down the hill, upon which the Leigh Vineries were built. Nothing remained of the Hanham Estate on Colehill by 1929, as shown by the Estate Map of that year.

The Bankes Estate still owned a considerable part of Colehill, but in the form of "islands", surrounded by property belonging to others. One of these abutted on to the original boundary on the east, extending from it to Leigh Lane, where an ancient boundary stone stood as recently as twenty years ago. Although much weathered, with the date inscribed on it indecipherable, the inscription "K Lacy" was still legible, and no doubt it was a "sister" stone to that still standing, near Elliott's Grave.

BELLS HOUSE (centre of left edge) with ONSLOW HOUSE (diagonally upwards, 35mm to the right) and HIGHLANDS (top left) seen from the air, from the north-west, in the 1950s. Giddylake runs through the trees, from top left to bottom right.

Chapter 3

HOLLOW WAYS AND HIGHWAYS

We have already noted three examples of surviving evidence of Colehill's past: the round barrows on Cannon Hill and in the grounds of St Michael's School, dating back more than three and a half thousand years; the main road through the village, which now carries such heavy traffic, following the line of a Celtic track; and the stone, near Park Homer Road, marking the ancient boundary of the Kingston Lacy Estate, going back to the times of the first Queen Elizabeth.

There is a fourth instance of our ancient heritage still to be seen: the old pack-horse tracks, dating back at least 300 years, on the southern and western slopes of the hill. Pack-horses, as a means of transport, were disappearing from the scene towards the end of the seventeenth century in favour of wagons and coaches; this enables us to date these sunken roads with some certainty.

The pack-horse tracks which led from the ford over the River Stour at Canford up to Colehill suggest that John of Gaunt's House at Canford, now Canford School, was the hub of a considerable trade. Tracks across Canford Heath connecting the ford with the coast, especially in the neighbourhood of Poole Harbour, had carried, from very early times, a regular and extensive traffic from across the Channel with the French ports, even from those as far south as Bordeaux.

The hooves of countless horses passing up and down the hillside at Colehill loosened the sandy soil and the winter rains scoured it away until the surface of one of the tracks, now a road, Beaucroft Lane, is today more than 25 feet below the level of the ground on each side.

About half-way up the hillside, the soil becomes firmer and at the summit it is nearly as hard as stone in dry weather. The track would move aside whenever it became muddy on this harder ground, and because of this, it soon became indefinite and widespread. Further traces of the main track have thus become obliterated, but the track down Beaucroft Lane is well defined. The surface was macadamised and the rain water diverted to gutters at each side in 1941, but the road remains in a deep hollow along its middle section. Beaucroft Lane and another road leading up over the hill, Leigh Lane, survive as sunken roads and evidence of the old trails.

When the railway was built in 1847 and a bridge subsequently provided to replace the original level crossing in Leigh Lane, the works obliterated all evidence of the horse tracks at the bottom of the hill. But as recently as 50 years ago, the route could be traced beyond Leigh Road, a well-defined track as much as three feet below the surface of the field on each side. It led, presumably, to the ancient ford, which became submerged in the deeper water when the weir was constructed, late in the nineteenth century, to provide water power to drive the turbines for the new mansion in Canford Park.

This trade route appears to have been eventually abandoned in favour of one through Wimborne, for there still exist remnants of at least one other well-worn track leading to Colehill from that direction.

This track was the subject of a conversation recorded by a local historian, Reginald Willcox, in 1933. He wrote:

"I was examining the obvious remnant of one of these tracks alongside Rowlands at Glen House, when an old man, observing my interest, told me that when he was a small boy, that deep-cut track was the only road out of Wimborne in that direction. There were no houses on either side of Rowlands or on St John's Hill, nor any of the large houses above Glen House. In summer, the hillside was all fields of waving corn. The one and only road from Wimborne came over what is now the entrance or gateway to Bucklers Hard and turned into a natural chine at the foot of the garden of Glen House and thence wound upwards through where the large houses now stand. My informant was then 82 years of age."

This conversation, then, records the scene as it was 150 years ago on the western fringe of Colehill. We have confirmation from other sources that the upper part of the track was filled in when the houses were built. The recollections of an old gardener at Onslow House are of the remnants of the track being filled in where it crossed the top of a field on that estate. This hollow way is clearly shown on both the 1895 and 1928 Ordnance Survey maps, diverging from the modern road at the foot of Rowlands, passing behind the houses up the hill, and emerging again to run parallel with Rowlands at Glen House; it can still be seen beside Rowlands Hill, and again in the continuation of the sunken track at the top of the hill, alongside the footpath leading to Tower Lane.

As to the route of the track at the bottom of the hill, the 1811 first edition of the Ordnance Survey map shows the road running due west to the River Allen, where there would have been a ford. Two separate maps, both dated 1775, confirm this route, running from East Borough, in Wimborne, over the river, or rather, through it, and continuing up the hill to Rowlands. A street map of Wimborne shows this as far as the Allen, labelling it "Old Road". And the continuation on the eastern side of the river is, indeed, the "Old Road" recorded by the Woodward Survey of the Kingston Lacy Estate, which we have already noted, and joining the old "Bell Lane".

There is no doubt that the pack-horse tracks, apart from their use as legitimate trading routes, were also in common use for smuggling. Another local historian, the Rev Arthur Stote, Vicar of Colehill, wrote in the Parish Magazine in 1931:

"But why *Smugglers* Lane? I can understand our worthy sub-postmaster's disgust at being made to live in such a low neighbourhood as that now occupied by the Vicarage, but I personally like living in Smugglers Lane! I remember an old parishioner telling me that his father, who lived at Dean's Grove, actually saw the smugglers with their ponies and panniers conveying kegs along the lane that passes the Vicarage, and that some of his father's labourers used to have a keg left on their doorstep for looking out for the Preventive Men whilst pretending to cut the hedge! So

Smugglers Lane records parish history."

It still does so, sixty years later, for what seems to have been a campaign by some of the residents to change the name of the road was unsuccessful.

Part, at least, of Smugglers Lane seems to have been known as "Batchelor's Drong" more than two hundred years ago, according to the Kingston Lacy archives. Other names that have disappeared over the years are also revealed by the Woodward Survey of the estate. Doll Davy's Lane was the name for part of what we call Dogdean. We have already noted other names which have vanished, such as Middle Bound Way and Bell Lane. Studicks Hill Road was the name given to a trackway more or less parallel to the Middle Bound Way, and to the north of it, approximately on the line of our modern Cobbs Road and running on to "Merry Field Hill", with the "Great Barrow", one of the tumuli now within the confines of the playing fields of St Michael's School, on its southern side.

Perhaps the end of the track which now emerges into Smugglers Lane at the top of the hill, is another remnant of the ancient Studicks Hill Road. A study of the Woodward map reveals other variations of place names. Giddy Lake, spelt as two words, must have been some sort of pond, at least, shown towards the bottom of Burts Hill, on the Wimborne side, and not the name of the steep, winding track, which now ascends the hill from this point. Coneygar, which must have been the home for rabbits (and perhaps still is), split up into two meadows, Great Coneygar and Little Coneygar, as well as Coneygar Coppice, lay between Bell Lane and Beaucroft Lane. Vincecombe is another vanished name, sited near the top of Beaucroft Lane. The name is shown prominently on the map, and may have represented a farm, or some other substantial building or buildings. Peaks was the name of a meadow, opposite the "New Plantation"; and Peaks Hedge "Cotage" was sited nearby.

The "Great Barrow" recorded on the Woodward map is clearly one of the tumuli now in the grounds of St Michael's School, but it is difficult to place the "Little

Barrow" on the modern map. "Tumps" are marked at intervals along the Middle Bound Way, and these may have been mounds to signify, in somewhat barren, featureless country, the dividing line between the Bankes and the Hanham Estates. Gravel "Pitts" are shown, roughly on the site of the present-day Cobbs Road.

We have digressed rather from the matter of roads, but while on the subject of the Woodward Survey, it is of interest to note that, in 1775, at least one of our local hostelries was in business, John Barnes holding the lease of "The Horns Ale House". Between the Horns and Dogdean, the upland was called Gooks Hill. On the opposite side of the road from the Horns, and down the hill towards Smugglers Lane, a plot was leased to Samuel Burden "with the Brick Kiln". This early reference to brickworks on Colehill cannot be identified with either of the later works, those of Cobb and Coombes, although it was not very far from either. A deep hollow behind Chapel Cottage, beside the track running up from Burts Hill, along the boundary of St Michael's School playing fields towards the Church, is suggestive and may have been the clay-pit for this early brickworks; it certainly indicated a general area of suitable clay in the vicinity. The land down towards Giddy Lake, on the other hand, seems to have lent itself more to horticulture, with two nurseries situated on these slopes.

Returning to the topic of thoroughfares, the main highway between Wimborne and London, via Ringwood, passing below the hill, is, of course, of greater antiquity than the smugglers' tracks. We know it as Leigh Road as it passes to the south of the village, and remember it as part of the A31 trunk road, before the opening of the Wimborne by-pass a few years ago. It probably follows the line of, or very close to the line of, a Roman road. There was a carrier's service from London along it as far back as 1722. In 1758, the Ringwood, Longham and Leigh Turnpike was opened and the road thus became the responsibility of a Trust for the purposes of maintenance. The toll-gate was sited at Leigh Common. A regular coach ran from London in 1772.

Another mediaeval road ran from Uddens Cross, which was the junction of no fewer than nine roads, around the north of the hill, along the present-day Pilford Lane, to Holt.

All the roads that we have noted so far, with the exception of the prehistoric track along the spine of the hill, have been on the periphery of the village or leading up to the hill. The only other tracks shown by the 1811 Ordnance map on the hill itself were Northleigh Lane, Greenhill Road, Colehill Lane, Pilford Heath Road, and the section of Middlehill Road below the school, an early road "improvement" to give an easier gradient for wheeled traffic on the ascent from Little Canford. We must remember that all these roads were no more than tracks and remained so for a further 120 years or more, until the comparatively recent surfacing with tarmacadam.

The last line of communication to complete the scene by the middle of the nineteenth century was the coming of the railway, the Southampton and Dorchester Railway, in 1847. Within 120 years, this had gone, "axed" as a result of Dr Richard Beeching's report. Since there was never a station in the village, the railway was scarcely of any immediate importance to Colehill. However, the line ran below the hill, to the north of and roughly parallel to the A31 road. Parts of the track-bed are still visible, still crossed by the Northleigh Lane bridge; and the original crossing-keeper's cottage, now a private residence, survives, a short distance away, in Leigh Lane.

TRACKBED OF THE OLD RAILWAY and the Northleigh Lane bridge, 1989.

GENERAL SIR EDWARD GREATHED, of Uddens. Print of a charcoal study for a portrait by George Richmond, when Sir Edward was a Colonel, circa 1860.

JEMIMA BOULGER, later Mrs. Charles Webb, in a portrait of about 1863.

CHARLES WEBB, of Northleigh House, circa 1867.

SHOOTING PARTY, circa 1867. The figures include Tom Rawlins, James Hall, his butler, Haines, his coachman, Aunt Annie Rawlins, Charles Webb, Parson Bullen, Joe Neall, Joseph, the head keeper, Evelyn, Mr. King, Grantley Berkley, General Murchell and Rev. Heath.

THE WEBB FAMILY, outside south front of Northleigh House, c. 1875. Left to right are Charles, Aunt Lily, with his children, Lilian and Harry and their nurse, Maria Kail.

COLONEL LEOPOLD PAGET, of Park Homer House, inspiration for the building of St. Michael's Church, from a sketch by Berry Dallas, 1872 (reproduced from *Our Journal at Winterbourn St. Martins* published by Dorset Natural History & Archaeological Society.

Chapter 4

THE VILLAGE TAKES SHAPE

Round about the middle of the nineteenth century, Colehill would still seem to have been an expanse of largely uninhabited heathland, with, as we have seen, some cultivation on its western and northern fringes, a network of trackways covering the hill, and a scattering of humble, mud-built cottages with thatched roofs, occupied by the handful of people who constituted the population. Some of these cottages survive to this day, having been restored before they could fall into decay; others have been converted into more substantial, brick-built dwellings, such as those in Smugglers Lane, near the Post Office. But many have vanished, several within the last thirty years, the victims of weather and neglect, having fallen into disrepair, and then been abandoned.

The Wimborne Tithe Map of 1847 shows the various dwellings; one, long since gone, was occupied by Mary Sweetapple and stood, rather aptly, in the orchard of the later residence, The Further House, now known as Joldwynds: that section of Leigh Lane, now relegated (or elevated!) to the status of a bridleway, was then known as Sweetapple Lane. Mary Sweetapple, aged 70 at the time, is recorded in the 1841 Census, living with her 65-year-old sister, Ann. Ann is named as the head of the house in the 1851 Census, by which time, curiously, twelve years have been added to the ages of both women, and they have a washerwoman, Elizabeth Thorn, living with them. A neighbouring property was occupied by John King, a master bricklayer, and his family, among whom was a son, Robert, aged 25, also a bricklayer.

The track was still known as Sweetapple Lane at the time of the 1871 Census, although Mary no longer lived there, and had probably died. At a later date, it was called Lower Road, Further Lane, and indeed, other alternatives. Bondskins, perhaps a corruption of Bob King's, was one variant. Bob, no doubt the son of John King, apparently occupied the same neighbouring cottage, in which his parents had lived, and which has also vanished. A plot shown on a plan attached to a legal document of 1886, on the western side of Leigh Lane, then known as "Lower Road", is marked "Land held for lives vested in King's representative", and probably indicates the site of this cottage.

The 1847 Tithe Map also shows the bull-pits on Rowlands Hill (already recorded on an earlier map, the Wimborne street map of 1775), Cobb's brick kiln at Greenhill Road and the hop gardens in Beaucroft Lane as well as the newly constructed railway line.

The Tithe Map also records a plot of land in Northleigh Lane, now occupied by what was once the coach house of Northleigh House, as "Pot Kiln Close (i.e. meadow) and Barn", owned by Edward Castleman, the Wimborne lawyer and railway promoter, in the occupation of Henry Habgood.

A composite picture of the village in the middle of the nineteenth century emerges from the Tithe Map, and documents such as Kelly's Directories and the Census Returns, which record the wide variety of occupations followed by the inhabitants. Among those listed in the 1841 Census are the brickmaker, John Cobb, then aged 50, George Thorne, described as a yeoman, living at Pilford, Thomas Stiles, a shoemaker in Merryfield, Samuel Stickland, a turner in Leigh Lane, and Frederick Welch, a horse dealer, who also kept the Horse and Jockey inn, precursor of the much later Jockey House hostelry at Leigh Common. Reuben Hopkins was licensee of the Barley Mow, Stephen Frampton was a leather dresser, and the Croom family followed three different trades, William, the father, being a turner, and his sons, John, a cordwainer, and Edward, a tailor.

Kelly's Directory for 1848 lists a rush dealer and basket maker at Little Lonnen, and a wheelwright named Thomas Dacombe in Leigh Lane. There was a sawyer, two bricklayers, one of whom, James Wareham, of Merryfield, was also engaged as a farmer, and two other farmers, Bowling at Little Lonnen, and John Hatchard, at Dean's Grove, where he farmed 350 acres, and employed sixteen men, six boys and six women.

Little *London*, as an alternative to Little *Lonnen*, seems to have been used throughout much of the nineteenth century. It has been suggested that "London" was the original – the Census of 1841 uses this form, and this spelling survives as late as the returns for 1881 – and that Dorset speech converted it to the modern version. Yet another variant, Little *Lunnen*, appears in the Electoral Registers for 1886 and later.

Occupations recorded in the 1851 Census include agricultural labourers, cattle dealers, flour mill labourers, chimney sweeps, cordwainers, carpenters, bricklayers, grooms, vets, plumbers, painters and sawyers. There was even a "Railway Servant" and a lawyer. Charles Harding kept "The Horn*e*s Inn", where he was succeeded by Samuel Smith; and Thomas West, born in the Cape of Good Hope, was licensee of the Barley Mow. J. Cutler farmed ten acres in Long Lane. John Cobb, the owner of the brickyard, had died and the business, employing two men, was now run by his widow, Elizabeth, to be eventually succeeded by the son, David, then aged 35. George Cobb was a bricklayer and ironmonger, and another Elizabeth Cobb was a dressmaker.

A native of Newfoundland, Dacombe, living in Holt Lane, was a knitter of stockings. Newfoundland, Britain's oldest colony, was closely connected with Dorset, in particular Poole, through the rich fisheries on the Grand Banks. Three Ha*p*good families are mentioned, living at Broomhill – whether these are related to the earlier or later Ha*b*goods is uncertain, but the spelling of names in the nineteenth century Census returns was not always completely reliable. Among other entries of interest are Elizabeth Cole, a laundress, Edmund Evans, a basket maker, Moses Welch, a labourer, and William Bellows, of Turnpike House at Leigh Common, who collected the tolls, in succession to James Fancy. Henry Freeborne was an agricultural labourer, maybe a descendant of that Freeborne whose "Slop" was a landmark on the Kingston Lacy Perambulation 75 years earlier.

Thomas Foster farmed 90 acres at Pilford Farm in 1861. On the other side of the hill, Joseph Dinneth had become the innkeeper at the Horse and Jockey, and James Miller was the gatekeeper at the nearby Leigh Turnpike Gate House, combining his duties there with his other rather apt occupation as a miller's labourer. The first record of Park Homer House appears in the 1861 Census, when it was occupied by John Niell, the 70-year-old manager of the gas works, who also found time to farm seventeen acres.

The 1868 edition of Hutchins's county history paints much the same overall picture of Colehill:

"... a few little cottages are scattered here and there around the hill; but it has nothing worthy of notice. A wood called 'Pleasure House Plantation' marks the site of an observatory, or summer-house, built by Sir William-Thomas Hanham, commanding an almost unbounded and most delightful prospect. Colehill belongs partly to the Hanham estate and partly to Mr Bankes."

The Pleasure House Plantation is shown on the 1875 Hanham Estate map, lying behind North Leigh House on Northleigh Lane and extending almost as far as Beaucroft Lane. A document in the Hanham archives, dated 1881, shows that the Plantation covered more than ten acres.

John Hutchins, the Wareham clergyman, produced the first edition of his celebrated work on Dorset in 1773. The third edition, corrected and augmented by William Shipp and James Whitworth Hodson, was produced between 1861 and 1874, the part relating to Colehill appearing in 1868. However, the survey for it had clearly been completed some years earlier, as no mention is made, under the entry for Hampreston, of three prominent buildings which we know from other sources had then been built on that part of Colehill, one of the big houses, Park Homer, certainly by 1861, and the School at Middlehill, in 1865; nor, indeed, of the original Methodist Church, which must have been standing at that time.

Neither is it recorded that a considerable part of Colehill was owned by the Uddens Estate, including, significantly, that portion where the school had been erected. This part of the village then lay, of course, not in the parish of Wimborne, but in that of Hampreston. Sir Edward Harris Greathed, bearing the same names as his father, had succeeded to the Estate in 1840, but at the time of which we write, he was far distant from Uddens, serving with distinction in India at the time of the Mutiny. He was a Lieutenant-Colonel and commanded the column which relieved Agra.

Readers familiar with the Sherlock Holmes stories of Conan Doyle will perhaps remember seeing mention of this soldier's name in *The Sign of Four*. His exploits at Agra were much celebrated at the time, certainly locally and probably nationally. A Grand Triumphal March, with a Cornet Solo, was composed by an unknown musician – "Homage to Colonel Greathed" – to mark the feat. In his absence, his home, Uddens House, was occupied by the Deputy Lieutenant of Dorset, Thomas Evans. Sir Edward had risen to the rank of Major-General and had returned to Uddens by the time of the 1871 Census, when he was aged 58. He had presumably retired from the Army at the time of the 1881 Census. His wife, Charlotte, was then 44, and there was an eight-year-old daughter, Elizabeth, who grew up to inherit the estate. At that time, there was a staff of fifteen servants.

The responsibility for the maintenance of the roads, apart from the turnpikes, lay with the waywardens of individual Tythings, until 1863. Colehill lay partly within the Tything of Leigh. The Wimborne District Highway Board was constituted in 1863, and took over the waywardens' responsibilities for the next thirty years until the coming of local government in its modern form.

Colehill was about to be transformed completely, and although very much dependent on its close neighbour down the hill, assume an identity of its own as a community. The latest fashion among those professing some medical knowledge was to promote the health-giving properties of pinewoods, to be followed in due course by the desirability of living near the sea. "Smell the 'Ozone'" became the prescription for all manner of ills for that and succeeding generations! The pinewoods attracted a number of well-to-do residents to Colehill, as well as to places such as Bournemouth. As late as 1918, indeed, a London doctor was advising a patient, suffering from tuberculosis, to move to this district, with its pine trees – and that is what brought Frank Baldwin and his family to Colehill, to start his bakery business.

Burrow's *Pocket Guide* to Wimborne Minster, produced in the early years of this century, comments that "the residential portion now stretches away, amidst picturesque surroundings, towards Colehill, where the pine woods rival those of Bournemouth ... Land and houses on Colehill, adjoining the Urban District, are particularly sought after, the sites being healthy and commanding fine views".

The Wimborne area particularly attracted the "new" aristocracy when one of their number, Sir Josiah John Guest, the ironfounder from Dowlais in Glamorgan, and father of Sir Ivor Bertie Guest, first Lord Wimborne, chose Canford as his seat. Another factor in the new development was the financial crisis of 1866, when the shortage of "real" money resulted in the heathland, of little value for agriculture or the extraction of minerals, being sold for building development. This applied equally to Colehill, as borne out by advertisements in the local press, as it did to the Bournemouth area.

They built their great houses up the hill from Wimborne: Onslow, erected in 1884 for the Truell family, Bells House (taking its name from the succession of large pasture meadows, Bells, Great Bells and the Ringing Ground, running down to the banks of the River Allen, owned by the Hanhams, who indeed remained ground landlords for the house and other neighbouring properties, on long leases), Audrey's, Highlands, Beaucroft, Park Homer, Northleigh, Rowney, Olivers; and filled them with their families and their servants.

Northleigh House was built in 1862 for Charles Webb, who married six years later, and it became the family home for more than thirty years. He was related to a Scottish aristocratic family, the Naesmyths of Posso, among whom was James Naesmyth, the inventor of the steam hammer. In his will, Charles referred specifically to a "Presentation Clock belonging to my late brother James", who may well have been the inventor himself. Webb's second Christian name, Nasmith, appears to be an anglicised version, possibly inherited from his mother, but the spelling of this name varied widely, even for the same individual. The name was bestowed on the eldest son, known usually as Harry. He seems to have used the form "Nasmith", but was christened "Naesmythe", and in his father's will is called "Naysmith". Webb's family was served by a staff of nine servants, including a gardener and a French governess, Marie Leverot, and George Cross, the coachman, who lived with his family in separate accommodation, above the coach house, on the opposite side of the road.

An old map of the surroundings, dating from Webb's time at Northleigh, spelt as one word at that time, reveals that Northleigh Lane at that time joined Wimborne Road some considerable distance west of its present junction at the Fiveways; after the realignment, there remained, for some while, a triangle where Beechwood now stands. The same map marks an "old bank", which must have been an ancient boundary, running across Hanham's Pleasure House Plantation, branching off from Northleigh Lane, on its western side, near the top of the hill.

Charles Webb was keen on shooting and was apparently fond of entertaining: some evidence of this exists in the form of a rough inventory of the contents of the cellar when he died. This itemises in *dozens* of bottles, twenty of Port, thirteen of Sherry, eleven of Claret and seven of Burgundy. Four dozen each of Champagne, Brown Sherry, Sauterne and Hock, three and a half of Madeira, two of Whisky and one of Brandy, plus "a few odd bottles" complete the list. A valuation of the entire contents of his house, made a year or two before his death, for insurance purposes, included an item for £300 for Wines and Liquors, in a total of £3,100. £170 of this total was represented by harness, saddlery, carriages, etc. Among the items listed in his other belongings was a "Musical Boy".

Webb died in 1892, leaving a 45-year-old widow, Jemima (or Mimi or, according to his will, Minnie), three sons and two daughters. His eldest son, Harry, followed him into the malting business. There were malthouses in Poole Road, Wimborne, and at no fewer than seven other addresses in the town, and among the suppliers of malt and barley was Thomas Rawlins, his neighbour down the hill at Colehill, who had several acres under cultivation.

A childhood pastime of Harry, and one of his brothers, had been to roll the great stone balls from the gateway of Northleigh House down the hill. When the eighth Baronet Naesmythe of Posso, Sir Douglas, died, the line became extinct, and Harry, the senior surviving member of the family, who lived to be 94, changed his surname, and so the later generations of "Webbs" have been known as Naesmythe of Posso.

Charles Webb originally owned only the land occupied by the house and its extensive grounds on the western side of the lane. Over the years, he acquired the meadows belonging to John Joyce on the opposite side of the road, and considerably more land from Phelips Brooke Hanham, and by the time of Webb's death, the Northleigh Estate had spread to include all the land between Leigh Lane and Northleigh Lane, known at that time simply as the road leading from Leigh Common to Colehill, from the railway line at the bottom of the hill to Kyrchil Lane at the top. The Conveyance from Hanham recites the names of "the several closes or parcels of land situate near Park Homer and Cole Hill": Higher and Lower Ten Acres, Higher Mansels and Mansels (with withey bed, both forming part of Leigh Farm), Hunt's Plot and Long Lane Ground.

There was a delay of several months following Charles Webb's death before Northleigh was sold, while the lawyers sorted out an involved family quarrel over finances. Much of the Northleigh Estate, including the house, was sold to Dr John Wiblin in 1894 and he is recorded as living there in the electoral register of 1900. However, by then, ownership of most of the estate had passed to Lieutenant-General John Glyn, a veteran of the Crimea and Ashanti, and his wife, Dame Ellen. She, it seems, insisted on living in a house "of a standard to conform to the style of living to which she was accustomed". Glyn was the second son of Carr Glyn, Rector of Witchampton; Mary, a daughter by the Rector's second wife, married Edward Greathed, of Uddens. This linking of two great Dorset families no doubt accounts for the fact that, according to Kelly's Directory for 1899 and the electoral register of the following year, Lieutenant-General John Glyn was living at Uddens House, and moved from there to Northleigh. He would be knighted in 1911.

Apart from the area sold, first to Wiblin and then to General Glyn, other plots came into the ownership of Stevenson and Mrs Dibben, and Glyn was negotiating for the purchase of the "Long Lane Ground". The area to the south, on the meadows known as Lower Ten Acres, Mansels and Lower Mansels, was bought by Josiah Quertier, and on these he started his Leigh Vineries. There was a proposal to drive a new road, linking Northleigh Lane and Leigh Lane, along the northern boundary of Quertier's land, but this never materialised.

The electoral register for 1883 gives Tindal Atkinson as residing at "Bells"; the next register, compiled in 1886, records Herbert Cross at that address; both entries refer, presumably, to Bells House.

At least three of the larger properties had separate coach houses, that for Northleigh standing within the grounds of the house, and being subsequently replaced by a larger building on the opposite side of the road, that for Bells within the grounds of the house, which also took in the present Colehill cricket ground, and that for Beaucroft also within its extensive grounds. All three coach houses survive and have been converted into substantial private dwellings, the Bells coach house now known as "High Hanger" while the third of these is the aptly named "Beaucroft Mews".

Mrs Lees, who owned Beaucroft, was born Bernarda

Turnbull, in Mexico. She married Thomas Lees, who was the owner, jointly with his cousin, of a cotton mill in Lancashire – the Lees and Wrigley Mill, at Oldham. She was widowed, at the age of 37, in 1879, and brought her family – five daughters and a son – to Dorset apparently on account of the health of her son, Elliott, who suffered from asthma.

The son was created a Baronet in 1897, and lived at Lytchett Manor. The present Baronet, Sir Thomas Lees, is the great-grandson of Mrs Lees. Among the bequests made in her will, she remembered her servants and specifically named Alfred Moore, her coachman, Sarah Pavey, her maid, and Towena Randal. She also had a dairyman and a carter, who lived in two cottages, beside each other, on the opposite side of Beaucroft Lane, now combined into one spacious single house. This was known, at one time, as Beaucroft Dairy Cottage.

Colonel Paget, who moved to Park Homer in 1865, had aristocratic family connections, his uncle having been the first Marquess of Anglesey. He provided substantial "cottages" for both his coachman and gardener. Although the big house was demolished within a century, the cottages survived, one of them for only a few more years, but the other still stands, and would today itself be described as "a highly desirable residence.".

The Colonel seems to have been a considerate employer, in an age when there were not many such, and distinctions between the classes were very sharply drawn. He was also a public-spirited individual, being the inspiration behind the building of the first Anglican Church, and inaugurating an endowment fund to raise the necessary capital for it. The 1871 Census records him, aged 46, a Royal Artillery officer, on half-pay, living with his wife and family, with a staff of twelve servants. Three sons are listed, Lennox, Ralph and Mark, the youngest, aged seven. There were five other sons and a daughter, Adelaide, all presumably older, who had apparently left home or were away at school at the time of the Census. The servants included Janet Beane, a governess, two grooms, Henry Gleed and Joseph Feasy, and a footman, Leonard Earley. Sarah Latimer was the laundress, and there were two couples named Burch in their service, of whom the men, James, the butler, and Charles, the gardener, were presumably brothers.

Paget's likeness is portrayed in two little sketches which appear in a pictorial diary, kept by Miss Berry Dallas, during a stay in Dorset in 1872. This has been published as *Our Journal at Winterbourn St Martins* and includes a record of a visit to the Pagets at Park Homer. The moustached Colonel is shown playing with a little dog.

Paget seems to have been something of a military historian, with a particular interest in the Napoleonic Wars. He delved into records of the Battle of Waterloo, fought ten years before he was born, to produce an item of family interest to the Greatheds, which remains in their archives. It seems likely that Colonel Paget and Sir Edward Greathed were well acquainted, both having served during the Indian Mutiny, when they may have met. Both held the same rank, Lieutenant-Colonel, at the time, although Paget was the younger man, by twelve years, and presumably received the injuries which caused his premature retirement during the campaign.

The name Leopold Paget appears twice in the electoral registers for both 1883 and 1886, under the Hampreston section, where his address is given as "Middle Hill House", and again in the Wimborne Minster list, where he is shown as living at Park Homer, Colehill. One wonders whether his unique position, living on the old parish boundary, gave the Colonel *two* votes, and whether he voted twice in the General Election of 1886!

Also dating from this era is the Middlehill School, built in 1865, and correctly described as the oldest surviving public building in the village. It was one of the 'Charity" schools which co-existed with the "National" and "British" schools of the time. It spent the first 70 years of its existence as a private school, only being taken over by Dorset County Council in 1935. The Greathed family, of Uddens, built the school on land belonging to the estate, and maintained it under a trust fund. Mary Greathed endowed the school, the first proceeds from this bequest being made in 1869; the school still benefits from the Greathed Endowment.

Middle Hill was written as two distinct words at this time, as were many other local placenames, Cole Hill being one obvious example, as well as Ham Preston and Long Ham. In 1894, the managers of the school entered into a 99-year lease with the estate at an annual rental of two shillings and sixpence. The weekly charge for schooling at this time was, presumably depending upon the age of the child, twopence or fourpence per pupil. 125 children, between the ages of three and fourteen, attended the school towards the end of the century.

Many other properties, on only a slightly less grand scale, were built at about the same time, in the mid-Victorian era. More modest dwellings, built towards the end of the century, included the small row of terraced houses called Holmsley Villas, in Middlehill Road, which until recently bore a plaque giving the building date as 1891. Paget Cottages, erected on part of the Park Homer Estate, were built in the same year, in the upper part of Leigh Lane, now Kyrchil Way. Pine View Villas, at the top of Greenhill, were built in 1901.

The Census returns of 1871 and 1881 continue to throw much light on the village and the occupations of the villagers. There was a School House, next to the Middlehill School, occupied by the mistress, Elizabeth Chaston, a widow. Her two daughters, Charlotte and Ann, lived with her, and both are described in the 1881 Census as pupil teachers, aged nineteen and sixteen respectively. The influx of new properties and their occupants naturally attracted a variety of trades to cater for their needs. We have already noted the existence of the brickworks, Coombes', in Smugglers Lane, and Cobb's, in Greenhill Road. The 1871 Census records John Coombes, aged 60, and his son George, and David Cobb, all listed as brickmakers. Ten years later, among the brickmakers listed is George Coombs, possibly from another family, as neither the spelling of his name nor his age tally with the earlier entry. Several other brickmakers are listed, presumably employees at the two kilns. No doubt the brickworks were kept very busy in the second half of the nineteenth century, supplying materials for the considerable building then going on. Coombes' was still in business up to the start of the Great War, but both of these works closed at that time, or soon after. The sites of both can still be identified, the hollows formed by the extraction of clay being clearly visible.

Cobb's works, where much of the brick kiln still survives, became Frank Peckham's farmyard. Indeed, the farm is known as Brickyard Farm, a rare case, in Colehill especially, of an industrial site reverting to agriculture. This kiln is marked on the 1847 Tithe Map, and so too is the cottage and garden plot owned and occupied by Cobb on either side of Cobbs Road, opposite the brickworks. Towards the end of its life, the kiln, still in the hands of the family, employed four men. They were engaged in digging the clay after the winter frosts and throughout the spring, and fired the kiln in summer, producing hand-made bricks and pipes for use in agriculture. The Cobb family gave up the business, which was carried on for a year or two more by the landlords, the Bankes Estate, before finally closing down in 1916.

Francis Guy was the blacksmith, aged 40 in 1871, and his son, Joseph Hardy Guy, who was to succeed him, was then fifteen, and described as a blacksmith's apprentice. Francis Guy was combining the occupations of blacksmith and innkeeper, probably at the Crown and Anchor in Wimborne, in 1881, and his two younger sons, George and Andrew, were also described as blacksmiths. The family had moved by 1886 and were living at Colehill. The elder son, Joseph, had married and had two sons, of whom the younger, Joseph Edward, then ten years old, was destined to become the village smith. The building of the blacksmith's workshop still stands in Colehill Lane, now in use as a store, although, after its working days, it saw service as the headquarters of the local Scout troop, and then as a meeting place for a group of musicians.

Henery Hall was a grocer at Glynville, and other trades dating from the later years of the old century were cloth-making, carried on at Lees's weaving shed at the corner of Tower Lane and Beaucroft Road, and the manufacture of candles at a factory at the junction of Beaucroft Lane and Wimborne Road.

Merryfield (or Merrifield, in the modern spelling), which remains an unmade track in this last decade of the twentieth century, seems to have been an important thoroughfare a hundred years ago. A map of the area around the church at the time it was built, dated 1892, shows the present cross-roads there as the junction of five tracks.

Colehill Lane then led, to the north, to "Little Lonnen and Broomhill" and to "Wimborne and Leigh" in the south. Smugglers Lane, to the east, led to "Park Homer", and in a westerly direction to "Merryfields". The fifth turning was in a north-westerly direction and was the road to Holt. A private house, Highwood, and its garden, now occupy the beginning of this route, but its continuation is the present-day track called Merrifield. That it, and neither of the modern roads, was shown as the road to Holt is an indication of its importance a hundred years ago. Three businesses, the village bakery, a builder, and a wheelwright's workshop, were situated in this road. The buildings all survive, now in use as private dwellings.

The 1881 Census records James Wareham, then aged 27, as the wheelwright, and the baker was 35-year-old William Barrett, father of Frank, then aged nine. William was familiarly known as "Billy Tweet", on account of his being in the habit of whistling as he worked. He was a lay preacher at Broomhill Methodist Church, and on his way home, would make a point of stopping at the Barley Mow to lecture its customers on the evils of drink. His visits could hardly have been welcome to the licensee, Joseph Long, who had taken over the inn from Jane Ivamy. Jane was the widow of George Ivamy, who kept the Barley Mow in 1861, when the Census records him as a grocer, beerseller and farmer of 30 acres. Stephen Ivamy, presumably his father, is described as a landed proprietor.

William Habgood was a neighbour of William Barrett. He was the builder of the Post Office, Paget Cottages, Holmsley Villas and Castle View, the name given to a short row of cottages in Lonnen Road, opposite the Post Office, with a view, not of a castle, but of Horton Tower. As a result of marriage between the families, at least three of a later generation living locally are great-granddaughters of *both* Barrett and Habgood.

The Barley Mow was kept by Long in 1881, and by Jesse Puttock five years later. Long had formerly been a baker at Leigh Common. It must be a matter of conjecture whether his bakehouse was the same as that of Henry Farrant some 40 years afterwards, and Ted Baldwin's 20 years later still. Joseph Parsons was a baker at Middlehill in 1881, as he had been for the past 40 years at least, and he was also engaged in the grocery trade for part of that time. His daughter, Ann, was a schoolteacher. Thomas Webb was a grocer at Pilford, perhaps an early forerunner of the Handy Stores of the present day. Frederick Bown, whose name was used to identify the crossroads at "Bown's Corner", was a carriage maker. William Coakes was described as a small farmer, and his son, John, who was to succeed him, was a twelve-year-old boy at the time of the 1881 Census. Many laundresses are listed at this time, and a whole neighbourhood of railway employees lived at Leigh Common, probably in the row of houses built by the London and South Western Railway Company at the bottom of Leigh Lane.

The character of the village was changing on the slopes of the hill down towards the Stour. The railway had been built in 1847 and traffic on it was increasing as the years passed, necessitating the doubling of the tracks in 1857. Four years later, the opening of the line from Salisbury, via West Moors, to Wimborne and beyond brought more trains along this stretch of line. Until the connection was made across Bournemouth from its old East Station to Branksome in 1888, the railway crossed by the Northleigh Lane bridge remained the main line from London to Poole, and until 1893, for trains from London to Dorchester and Weymouth.

With the opening of the "Direct Line", through Bournemouth and across Holes Bay, the railway at the foot of Colehill, the "Old Road" as the railwaymen called it, became a purely local line, carrying only the modest traffic between Bournemouth West and Brockenhurst, and on the branch, to Salisbury. However, it remained as a convenient relief route for main line trains during both wars and for holiday traffic at weekends during the summer in peace time.

The scene was being transformed, too, up the hill from the railway, with the erection of a large area of glasshouses, covering eight-and-a-half acres in all, along what was then the southern half of Leigh Lane. Leigh Vineries extended some distance back on the western side of the road, and specialised in the growing of tomatoes – "large quantities" were grown according to Kelly's Directory for 1935 – although grapes were also cultivated. The land, sold by Phelips Hanham to Charles Webb, and by his Estate to Quertier, was described as arable land, in the tenancy of William Munckton. Bourgaize and Co. are recorded as the owners of the Vineries in 1902, and the Quertier family seem to have been involved from the beginning. Josiah was living at Leigh, and had "property in Leigh Lane" in 1900; and John Cecil de Moulfreid Quertier, perhaps a son, appears in the annals later on, living at "Leigh Vineries" in 1915. John Quertier later made his home at Beechwood in Wimborne Road at the top of the hill; by a curious coincidence, the present owner of that house is descended from a family of nurserymen who, at the time the Quertiers started their enterprise, were in business far away, in what was then rural Middlesex and is now urban London.

Mackay's Glasshouse Properties Ltd. were among the last owners of the Vineries, Mackay finally selling the nurseries to George Cummings, who continued in business there until the 1960s. A row of houses had been built for employees, adjoining the glasshouses on the north, and remain conspicuous among the bungalows erected on the new "Vineries" housing estate which was built on the site when the glasshouses were demolished. Another survivor of Leigh Vineries is the house built for the manager, halfway along what remains of Leigh Lane. This became a grocer's shop for a short while, when the bungalows were first built, but was then split into two houses.

Its history has left Leigh Lane with the rather curious peculiarity in that, on its western side, which has a distinctly suburban appearance, the houses and bungalows are all numbered, while opposite, where the outlook remains still quite rural, with two surviving thatched cottages, the comparatively few properties are named rather than numbered.

Originally, Leigh Lane branched off from Leigh Road at the western extremity of Leigh Common, and its course across the common can still be traced, first as a footpath, as far as the steps which lead up to the roadway on the approach to the railway bridge, and then, on the other side of the modern road, as a track. The lane ran on, provided with a level crossing when the railway came, gradually climbing the hill. When the bridge was built, the level crossing became redundant, and Leigh Lane was diverted to its present course alongside the railway track to Northleigh Lane.

Given an "artifical" twist at its southern end, with something of an amputation, its northern half is now completely severed and has been renamed Kyrchil Way. Leigh Lane originally followed its sinuous way right to the top of the hill, emerging into Wimborne Road opposite the site of the Iron Church. Eventually it was decreed that the middle section, at the steepest point of the hill, should become, not a highway, but a bridle-track. Unfortunately, maps were still being produced, and many are clearly still in circulation, showing a through road. The author can remember helping to push a car trapped in the mud when its driver tried his luck up this section, and periodically, one is still called upon to give directions to motorists heading for Park Homer Road, three minutes' walk away, but a journey of about a mile and a half by car.

The insertion of a bridleway – though its official status

now is only a public footpath – in the middle effectively cut Leigh Lane into two halves, one on the Vineries Estate, and the other in the village at the top of the hill. On one occasion the Fire Brigade, having turned out to fight a blaze in one part of Leigh Lane, found itself in the wrong half. After this incident, in the 1970s, it was decided to rename the upper section, which still remains largely an unmade road, Kyrchil Way. Until it was removed in 1989, one could still discern the lettering giving the original name of the road on a sign attached to a house adjoining the motor garage premises in Wimborne Road.

LEIGH VINERIES, circa 1930, with the railway in the foreground. The thatched cottage between the glasshouses and the railway was later destroyed in an air raid.

THE IRON CHURCH, dubbed Trotman's Tin Tabernacle, circa 1890.

MIDDLEHILL SCHOOL Staff and pupils, in about 1895.

THE HORNS, date unknown, but probably from the early years of the twentieth century.

MR. J. GUY.

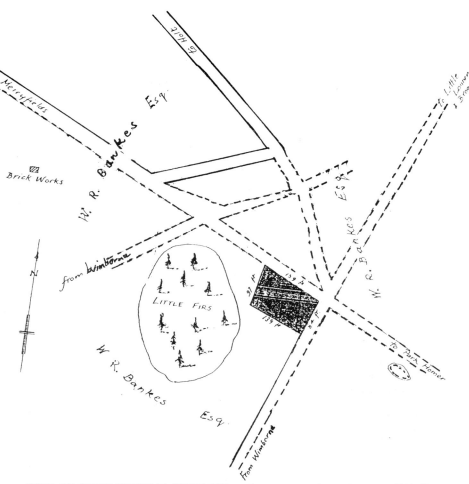

SITE OF ST MICHAEL'S CHURCH, at the cross-roads to the east of Little Firs, from the plan accompanying its land conveyance of 1892.

OPPOSITE

JOSEPH EDWARD GUY, a key player on the local football field and in the development of modern Colehill, reproduced from a yellowing newspaper cutting of about 1904. He was then captain of St Michael's Football Club: "'Joe' was born at Colehill twenty-eight years ago, and has a record of which few footballers can boast — he has only missed one match since the Club was started, and that was on account of an injury sustained whilst playing the previous Saturday. The Colehill skipper scales thirteen stone, and is five feet nine inches in height. He learnt his football at Southampton, where for three years he was numbered amongst the Highfield team, two years ago as goal-keeper and the third as right back. On returning to Colehill about four years ago, he became the leading spirit in the formation of the Saints, the members of which have so much confidence in him as to have selected him Captain for several years. His position at present is left back, and he is a good tempered player who can always be relied upon."

Chapter 5

THE PARISH IS CREATED

As we have seen, one of the first manifestations of an integrated community was the building of the village school at Middle Hill in 1865. However, this was preceded by the erection of a mud-built Primitive Methodist Chapel about ten years earlier. This stood in Lonnen Road close to where Four Wells Road now joins it, and was sometimes known as Little Lonnen Chapel. The building remained in use for worship until the completion of the present chapel, higher up the hill and on the opposite side of the road, in 1913. The Primitive Methodists continued to use the old building, certainly as late as 1917, for their Sunday School, and the newly formed Women's Institute was using it in 1919. The foundations of the old chapel remained visible for many years afterwards. The Primitives remained a distinct sect of the Methodists until the Union with the other two bodies in 1932.

There is considerable evidence to suggest that the Methodist connections with Colehill go back much further than 1855, indeed, to the early years of the century, when the "Dissenters" of Wimborne, under the leadership of Peter Hawke, were driven out of the town, and held their meetings at a cottage near Dean's Grove. It is a matter of conjecture whether or not the present-day "Chapel Cottage", set back from Burts Hill, down the hill from The Horns, is the original meeting place.

Marjorie Cailes, who produced an excellent booklet in 1988, celebrating the 75th anniversary of the "new" Methodist Chapel, gives a brief account of the early history of the Methodists locally in a preamble. John Parsons, a local preacher, was offered a house on Colehill for preaching at the end of the eighteenth century, but it was abandoned on account of so much opposition. Mrs Cailes continues: "There is constructive evidence that a cottage known as 'Chapel Cottage' near the Horns Inn was used as a 'Preaching Place'. Here Methodism was first started when in 1801 Peter Hawke came to Wimborne as a Tutor at the Grammar School, and with John Parsons, started to preach here and became the chief supporters of Methodism in the District." One or two members of the local congregation of the early years of this century have testified to having attended worship at the Cottage. "Mr Dacombe started Sunday School at Chapel Cottage," according to Dot Humphries (née Moody); and Mrs Dorcas Habgood "started Sunday School at Chapel Cottage and then it moved to a Chapel further down Lonnen Road before the present Chapel was built".

The coming of the Anglican Church was, as already noted, largely inspired by Colonel Paget, of Park Homer. Encouraged by the local clergy and Dr Hamilton, then Bishop of Salisbury, he read "The Afternoon Service" – presumably Evensong – every Sunday in the Middlehill Schoolroom, following the tradition originated by William Kingston, an author "of general literature", a former resident at Middle Hill. The services were well attended and, it seems, the church, in the broader sense of the word, was flourishing on Colehill in the late 1860s.

In the summer of 1880, Rev F. Trotman, Incumbent of Wimborne Minster, started open-air evening services on Colehill. Mrs Georgiana Paget, in her record, stated: "They were crowded, and a petition was signed by the neighbours – all poor people – praying Mr Trotman to get a Church built for them."

Thus the first Anglican Church, the Iron Church, funded by Colonel Paget, was built on Colehill. It could accommodate 200 people, and was sited in Wimborne Road, nearly opposite the present-day motor garage premises. Trotman agreed to officiate, and so, because of its construction, the building was dubbed locally as "Trotman's Tin Tabernacle". The church was opened in 1881 on the Feast of the Epiphany. The Wimborne Minster parish magazine for November 1888 has a short paragraph about the Colehill Harvest Festival, remarking that "the church was very prettily decorated" and that the helpers included Mrs Bernarda Lees and her daughters. The

Minster archives have a record of Christenings in 1889 at "Colehill Church". Both of these references would, in those years, have been to the Iron Church. It has long since gone, but the outline of its foundations remain clearly visible.

The Iron Church was apparently always regarded as a temporary measure, and within ten years, Paget's endowment fund had reached a figure which justified plans for the erection of a permanent building. Walter Bankes, of Kingston Lacy, made a gift of a plot of land and William Douglas Caröe was appointed as architect. He would become president of the Architectural Association and a notable designer of bishops' palaces and other ecclesiastical work. Colonel Paget, however, did not live to see the fruition of his labours, dying, after a very brief illness, in June 1892, before the building could be begun. Among a list of those who carried the work through were Mrs Lees, of Beaucroft, and the Truells, living at Onslow House.

Nine building firms tendered for the contract, which was awarded to Messrs Cornish and Gaymer, of North Walsham, Norfolk, at a price of £2,630. This firm, which presumably had to send some at least of its craftsmen 200 miles distant from their homes and to provide for their subsistence while working in Dorset, was able to complete the work at three-fifths of the price quoted by local firms. Some of the bricks used in the building were made at the Coombes works, a few yards away down the hill, these being more suitable than Cobb's products; but others came from further afield, arriving by train at Wimborne Station, whence they had to be hauled up the hill to the site. Major-General Robert Holt Truell, of Onslow House, met the cost of erecting the tower separately. John Wordsworth, Bishop of Salisbury, wrote, in September 1893, "handing over to the Spiritual care of the Vicar of Wimborne a specified portion of the Parish of Hampreston situated in the Vicinity of the new Church and including the School at Middlehill". The Church of St Michael and All Angels was dedicated by the Bishop on 11 December 1893 and consecrated in June 1895.

Successive curates of Wimborne Minster served St Michael's for the next seven years before the formation of the Ecclesiastical Parish of Colehill, from parts of the Parishes of Wimborne Minster, Wimborne St John's and Hampreston All Saints, in 1903.

The Local Government Act of 1894 created the system of Civil Parishes to administer, on a purely local level, matters in the public domain, taking over the civil functions of the Vestries. In that year Holt was constituted as a separate parish and divided into two wards, Holt and Colehill. Each was to elect one guardian and one councillor to the Wimborne and Cranborne Rural District Council, the next tier of local government, also created by the 1894 Act.

Two hundred electors of the Colehill Ward petitioned the County Council asking that Colehill should be constituted a separate parish, and the first meeting of the Holt Parish Council supported this initiative. A Dorset County Council Order, dated 5 November 1895, constituted the two villages as separate parishes and the Local Government Board confirmed this early in 1896. Colehill was on the administrative map of England.

A meeting was held on 9 March 1896 at St John's Schoolroom, Wimborne, to elect the first Parish Councillors for Colehill. Nine Councillors were elected, among them George Solly, later of Bells House, Francis Devenish Guy and Joseph Hardy Guy, familiar names in the unfolding history of the village.

The Parish Council held its first meeting at the Glyn Arms Coffee Tavern on 20 April 1896, and elected as their first chairman Robert Elcock. Elcock and John Smith, a local builder, were appointed as Overseers of the Poor of the Parish. The opening words in the council's first minute book were: "Late a Ward of the Parish of Holt and originally a portion of the Parish of Wimborne Minster in the Wimborne and Cranborne Union in the County of Dorset."

The Coffee Tavern, owned by Joseph Hardy Guy, was the only meeting place in the village at that date, and as its name suggests, supplied nothing in the nature of alcoholic drinks. It became the regular meeting place of the Council for many years, indeed until 1939.

The building, of corrugated iron, was originally sited in Lonnen Road, slightly further down the hill from its present junction with Four Wells Road, and the Methodist Chapel of that time, on land owned by Sir Richard Glyn, which extended from Lonnen Road to Green Bottom, and up the hill to Middlehill Road. His name is perpetuated in the area known as Glynville. The Coffee Tavern was physically moved at a later date to a fresh site in Colehill Lane, where it still survives, a little further down the hill from the old smithy.

One of the first duties of the Parish Council was to deal with just the same sort of complaint that had been brought before the Manor Court more than a century earlier; that was the question of "Certain persons exercising a greater right of pasturage on Leigh Common than they were entitled to". This same meeting of the Council also noted that the "London and South Western Railway had deposited compensation in one of the local banks when land from Leigh Common was taken to construct the Main Line". This had not been used for the general benefit of the owners of rights on the common. Another complaint (of the kind which never seems to go away) was that rubbish was being deposited in pits on the Common, such as Leigh Pond.

In October 1896, the Council endorsed a petition for the establishment of a Post Office, and a few months later they were negotiating with the Wimborne Gas Company for the provision of street lighting on certain roads, but the company were not to be allowed to deal in coal or lime. This was the start of a long-running saga: the Council were still debating the question of street lighting by gas in 1932! Even then, it was nearly another 30 years before the first lamps – lighted by electricity – appeared in the village. The Council minutes for the early part of 1897 record a long-running argument with the Rural District Council over the upkeep of the part of Long Lane between Merrifield and

Bown's Corner (taking its name from a resident of Long Lane), the junction with Smugglers Lane, which was described as "dangerous to the public".

The Rural Council declined to take over responsibility, but the Parish contended, quite correctly, that the lane was "one of the oldest roads on Colehill", and furthermore, had been under the control for many years of the late Highway Board, to whom the Rural District Council were successors.

Other matters which occupied the Council in their early deliberations were the provision of a recreation ground and a cemetery for the parish. The Council were trying to obtain a piece of land adjoining the railway line, close to the Water Works reservoir, for their playing fields in 1897.

Contemporary maps do not show this reservoir, but it may have adjoined the Gas Works of the time, to the north of Leigh Farm. In any case, they were unsuccessful in their efforts to obtain the land. The topic has cropped up from time to time ever since on Council agendas, but nearly a century later, there is still no recreation ground in the village.

The matter of the burial ground was quickly resolved. The Bankes Estate made an offer of a plot of land for the purpose, and the Council suggested two alternative sites, both near the Church. One was in Colehill Lane, running down to "The Slop" – the Marshfield houses now stand on this site – and the other was in Smugglers Lane, "on the summit of the hill, taking heathland on the north side of the road leading from Colehill Church to Coombs' brick kiln, and extending nearly opposite the old clump of firs, towards Merrifield".

Bankes declined to sell either of these, but suggested instead a field exactly opposite the Coffee Tavern in Colehill Lane. The Council agreed to accept this new site, but within six months, had changed its mind, and finally the idea of a cemetery in the village was laid to rest.

A minute on New Year's Day, 1900, quotes a letter from the Guardians to the effect that local recipients of Poor Relief would in future be paid at the Coffee Tavern, instead of at the workhouse in Wimborne.

It is in these early records of the Council that we find references to Curtis's Lane, the old name for the track running up from Burts Hill, near "The Horns", to St Audrey's – at the time of the 1775 Kingston Lacy Survey, plots in this area were leased to Christopher Curtis and William Curtis – and to "The Slop", that part of Smugglers Lane in the dip between the Church and the Post Office which, in those days before roads were surfaced, acquired a notoriety for its muddy condition. Dean's Grove, owned by Sir Richard Glyn, lay in the parish of Holt, until it was transferred to Colehill in 1897. We also learn that Little Lonnen was outside the parish, a surprising piece of information until we remember that the eastern part of the village, conforming to the land owned by the Uddens Estate, lay at that time in the parish of Hampreston. Even the village school lay outside the boundaries of the civil parish. Little Lonnen, Pilford, Glynville, Middle Hill and Canford Bottom were transferred from Hampreston to Colehill by a County Order in 1913.

It seems that earlier generations of bureaucrats were no quicker at rectifying anomalies of this kind than their modern counterparts. The re-drawing of the boundary in 1913 was very sensible, but we are still left with a civil parish extending to the River Stour in the south, and the River Allen in the west. On the other hand "The Barley Mow" is not in the parish, neither is Long Lane Farm, little more than five minutes' walk from Colehill Church: both lie within the boundaries of the civil parish of Holt.

The first meeting of the Wimborne and Cranborne Rural District Council was held on 4 January 1895, in the Board Room of the Union Workhouse at Wimborne. The new authority was formed from the old Wimborne and Cranborne Board of Guardians, whose attitude has been described by an earlier historian, George Watson, as "arrogant, with a churlish disregard for the welfare of employees and paupers whose interest they had been elected to guard". Watson's notes contain more in the same condemnatory vein, and he is scarcely less scathing in his comments on their successors in their early deliberations.

Little directly relating to Colehill emerges from the minutes of the first Council meetings. Robert Seymour, whose memory was, until a few months ago, perpetuated by a bench in Wimborne Road, opposite its junction with Beaucroft Road, was appointed Highway Surveyor in 1895. Later that year, there is a note of complaint from Hampreston Parish Council about the "dangerous position of part of the playground at Middlehill School", and about some trees at Park Homer House.

The 1885 Ordnance Survey map gives a clear picture of the village at that time. Virtually the whole of the top of the hill was tree-clad, the woodland extending all the way from Cannon Hill as far as Cobbs Road, in the west. Some clumps of trees are specifically named, such as Little Firs, near the site of the present Anglican Church, Stone Firs (possibly giving rise to a name in common usage later, Stoney Clump), Barrow Firs, marking one of the tumuli at the rear of our present St Michael's School, and Pleasure Firs, where Hanham's Observatory, noted by Hutchins, had stood. To the north of Smugglers Lane lay an area of marshland, on which now stand the Council houses, appropriately named Marshfield.

The area on the slopes north and south of the hill, and the western extremity of the ridge, was largely open fields, and the rest of the hilltop was heathland. Gravel, we have already noted, was being extracted as early as 1775, and the 1885 map indicates that this was being done on quite a large scale. Gravel pits are shown near the Middlehill School, at Glynville (there was also a sandpit here); in Wimborne Road, near the Post Office; at Merrifield; and along the fringes of the woods, on the west. Some of those in the area administered by the Parish Council, that is, in the western part of the village, were causing the councillors some concern in 1900, being a potential source of danger, and it was decided to write to Lodder, the agent for the Kingston Lacy Estate, requesting protection at the edge of the pits.

An old gravel pit is also marked, where Kyrchil Lane

now runs, and an old clay pit, beside Beaucroft Lane. Both Cobb's and Coombes's brickworks are recorded. Half a dozen prominent buildings are marked, of which only Middlehill School and three houses, Highlands, Beaucroft and North Leigh, remain. The two churches, the Anglican Iron Church and the first Methodist Chapel, have gone, as well as one of the big houses, Park Homer. The Coffee Tavern was resited in Colehill Lane.

Among the more interesting features of this 1885 map are that it marks the position of Elliott's Grave and also shows the old parish boundary, cutting through the middle of the village from north to south in a zig-zag line. This is shown as a four-foot boundary hedge, between the old parishes of Wimborne and Hampreston.

THE BARLEY MOW, circa 1906. The licensee's name, Steel, is just legible.

Chapter 6

INTO THE TWENTIETH CENTURY

Colehill, we have seen, entered the new century as a cohesive, but far from compact, community. The Census return of 1901 gives a total population of 1,005: but this was, of course, for the Civil Parish. The population of the Ecclesiastical Parish was about 700. There was a church and a chapel, both in the centre, yet keeping their distance from each other; the post office; the village "hall" of the time, known as "The Coffee Tavern"; the village school about half a mile away; the two public houses, the "Barley Mow" and the "Horns", both kept discreetly almost out of sight and very much at arm's length, at the bottom of the hill; and a trinity of "Squires", none of whom lived in the village.

The Post Office had opened in August 1897, with the 26-year-old Frank Barrett as Postmaster. He had opened a grocer's shop and bakery in a cottage in Wimborne Road, next to what became the laundry, and in later years, the motor garage, some little while before, when his father, William, was giving up his old bakery business in Merrifield. Frank moved his business along the road to the new premises when the Post Office was built.

Just as the Pagets were the founding fathers of the church, so other names, closely associated with the village, became influential in other spheres. Guy, Habgood, Dacombe, Welch, these names and others became prominent as the years passed. Some of these local families can, indeed, trace their ancestry back for generations. Among the jurors at the Court of Survey when the perambulation of the Kingston Lacy Estate was recorded in 1591 were Richard Habgood and Francis Daccum; Robert Habgood is mentioned in the annals of Wimborne in 1598; the name of John Habgood the Tanner occurs in 1602; Richard Habgood founded a Charity for the poor of Wimborne in 1642.

Henry Habgood was born in 1880, and as a boy of seven,

no doubt saw the great bonfire on Cannon Hill to celebrate the Golden Jubilee of Queen Victoria. When I met him, a nonagenarian with a remarkably clear memory, he was able to recall Colehill in the early years of this century. His father-in-law, Joe Guy, was the village blacksmith, who also owned the Coffee Tavern and was something of a musician, playing the bass and leading a "String Band". His full name was Joseph Hardy Guy, taking, for his second Christian name, his mother's maiden name, and was usually accorded his full appellation to avoid confusion with his son, also Joe. When he retired from the smithy and took over Colehill Farm, a little further down Colehill Lane, Joe Guy, junior, followed in his father's footsteps, and indeed those of his grandfather, Francis Devenish Guy, as the village blacksmith, and later, inheriting the "Tavern". He, too, was in the String Band, and played the violin. Habgood himself was a haulier by horse and cart. He carried coal to Coombes' brickworks in Church Hill (or Brick Hill or Smugglers Hill, alternative names at that time for the steep slope of Smugglers Lane); and he carried a different type of fuel, peat from the heathland, to fire ovens at William Barrett's bakery in Merrifield, and later, those of Frank Barrett at the new Post Office site.

The Habgoods and the Guys owed their ecclesiastical allegiance to the Methodist Church, not the Primitive Methodists of Colehill, but to the Wesleyans in the neighbouring hamlet of Broomhill, and both families were prominent in that church. Indeed, the "Colehill" String Band, or Orchestra, was in reality the "Broomhill" String Orchestra, which led the singing at the services of the Broomhill Methodists.

Ralph Habgood, Henry's son, in his admirable booklet marking the centenary of the Broomhill Church, likens the church music of the time to that described by Thomas Hardy in *Under the Greenwood Tree*. One of Hardy's musicians was paralleled by one of the Broomhill violinists, Albert Dacombe, who added a fifth string to his instrument.

The first performance of the String Orchestra on record

was in 1892, at Crichel, when the musicians included Henrietta Habgood, Ralph's mother, and the twelve-year-old Alf Dacombe, grandfather of John, the present Colehill Postmaster.

The Anglican Church gave its name to the football club, Colehill St Michael's or "The Mikes", for short, whose ground was a field in Tower Lane. The club, alternatively known as "The Saints", played in green and red shirts and was competing in the second division of the Bournemouth and District Junior League in the season 1903-04, with the younger Joe Guy as captain. Their opponents included Boscombe Athletic, better known today as the Football League side A.F.C. Bournemouth. Joe's father, Joseph Hardy Guy, and brother-in-law, Henry Habgood, were also among early Colehill footballers.

"Charlie" Hay, brother-in-law of Rev Cyril Kindersley, lived at Dean's Grove, moving to Rowney House some years later. A tall man, of aristocratic Scottish descent, related to the Marquis of Tweedsdale and the Earl of Erroll, he was the Registrar of Colehill. An enthusiastic sportsman himself, keen on hunting and shooting – he has been described as "a fine shot" – he was a great sponsor of both the football and cricket clubs. The latter also originated as a church club, Colehill St Michael's. Kindersley, appointed first Vicar of Colehill, in 1903, was. it seems, a fine cricketer and became the Club's first captain.

The origins of the club seem to stem from a cricket club associated with the Young Men's Bible Class, which played its first match on 25 June 1904. An account of the match records that their opponents, Broadstone, "gave us a decided beating. The best cricket shown was by Harry Frampton, who took most of the wickets, once performing a hat-trick. We had very bad luck in several of our best batsmen being caught out by marvellous catches, and what made it worse was that they were brought off by Colehill men who were playing as substitutes."

The same report records that the club members were practising three times a week.

The cricket ground was a field behind the Coffee Tavern in Colehill Lane, owned by Joe Guy, senior. The Guys, Habgoods and the Welch family, also related by marriage, all stalwarts of the Broomhill Methodist Church, were to become, down the years, the backbone of the Cricket Club, both as players and administrators.

Cricket must have been arranged on an ad hoc basis prior to the inaugural meeting of the Club, held on 17 April 1905. The founder members included Joe Guy, George Solly, of Bells House, and Frank Barrett, the postmaster and baker. Barrett, remembered for his perpetually drooping cigarette and nicotine-stained moustache and spectacles, and his "plus-fours", was elected treasurer of the Club, an office which he was to hold continuously for the next 33 years, until the outbreak of the second German war. He was also prominent in other village affairs, a Manager of the Middlehill School, a chorister and sidesman at St Michael's Church, a member of the Parochial Church Council, and latterly, a Churchwarden. He served on the Parish Council, too, for many years, and was its chairman for several of them. Barrett was also a favourite at local concerts, dressed in a "smock-frock" and rendering his songs with what has been described as a "broad, carroty 'Darset' accent".

The Cricket Club was supported from the outset by the local gentry. Solly was the first President, and the vice-Presidents elected at the opening meeting included Mrs Lees and members of the Glyn, Paget and Truell families.

The first recorded match, following the formal constitution of the club, was on 27 May 1905, against Crichel. This was an "away" match and a brake was hired at a cost of seven shillings and sixpence to carry the team there. It is a curious coincidence that the first recorded performances of both the Cricket Club and the String Orchestra should have been at that same hamlet. Perhaps the link was the builder from Crichel who erected some of our local houses around this period, and who brought a variation of the name of the hamlet, Kyrchil, to Colehill. William Habgood, known familiarly as "Warpy", and Joe Guy were in that early cricket team, and George Solly turned out for the

Club later that season. Among other names mentioned in those early matches was W. Freeborn. One wonders whether he might have been a descendant of that earlier "Freeborne", whose "Slop" was a boundary mark on the Kingston Lacy Perambulation Survey of 1775. Early opponents included clubs which, like Crichel, have long since ceased to function, Canford and Wallis Down among them. Solly was succeeded as President by Cyril Kindersley, the Vicar, in 1908, and by Charlie Hay the following year.

The Club seems to have experienced some difficulties in later years. No record appears in the Club Minute Book for 1910 and each of the Annual Meetings for the years between 1912 and 1914 was required to vote on some such motion as a decision "to keep the Club going" or "to field a team". There was some little financial trouble too, the treasurer reporting a deficit of £1.6s.6d. in 1913, the subscriptions, totalling £7.8s.,having been swamped by expenses. In 1914, the club was unable to play any home matches early in the season, the elder Joe Guy, the owner of the field, stating that it was not available before the end of June, when, presumably, the hay harvest would have been gathered. It was decided to seek another ground, but the problem was shortly to be resolved by the start of what turned out to be a much grimmer contest than a cricket match.

Returning to the memoirs of Henry Habgood, he recalled that the "village used to be run" by Mrs Paget, of Park Homer, and Mrs Lees.

Habgood was related by marriage to John Cobb, owner of the brickworks at Greenhill Road, then known as Horns' Hill. These had been started about 1840, by Henry Cobb, the great-grandfather of David Cobb, the chiropodist, who also ran a hairdressing business in a timber building at the side of his house in Wimborne Road until the 1970s.

The area around Green Bottom and across what were the playing fields of the school, now largely built over with the Library, the Memorial Hall and the supplementary classroooms for the expanding Middlehill School, was given over to the extraction of gravel in the early years of this century. The pits are recalled in such names as Quarry Corner and Quarry Road.

At least two theories have been offered as to the origin of the name Merrifield. One version suggests that it was, simply, the field in which "merries", a local term for a type of sweet cherry, were grown. The harvest was taken once a year along the track known as Dark Hollow and up the hill to a field opposite the Horns Inn where the fruit was sold at the open-air "Merrimarket". The alternative maintains that Merryfield derives from "Meerfelde", meaning boundary field. Supporting this version is the proximity of Merrifield with the ancient boundary of the parish of Holt.

Jenny Down, otherwise known as "Jane Down", "Ginny Down" or "Stoney Clump", was an open area, partially covered with heather, and with some tiny saplings, where the children of the village played, and where donkeys grazed. Male donkeys were familiarly known as "Jacks" and the females as "Jennies", which gave rise to the local name for the area. The trees grew to form quite a substantial wood by the early 1970s. A great number of these were felled when St Michael's School was built and its playing fields laid out. So the wheel has turned full circle here, as once again, the children of the village (and others) play their games on part, at least, of the old Jenny Down. A small group of trees remains on the playing fields, all that is left of Stoney Clump, still known locally as "Soldiers' Ring", marking, according to the traditional legend, the burial ground of some of Cromwell's troops. Colehill Pond nearby, adjacent to Cobbs Road, was the venue for skating and ice hockey in season, but this has vanished without trace with the coming of the Beaucroft School. The field near Giddylake where the Colehill Cricket Club now play was used for grazing at the turn of the century.

Among other place and street names familiar to residents of Colehill at that time were Glyn's Hill, where General Sir John Glyn lived at Northleigh House, in what is now Northleigh Lane, and Coffee Tavern Road (although whether this meant Lonnen Road or Colehill Lane is not clear). "Doll Davy's Lane", of the eighteenth century, had become "Doll Davids Lane" and was not to become Dogdean until several more years had elapsed.

The Education Act of 1902, among other provisions, ironed out various anomalies with regard to elementary schools and ordained that managers should be appointed to oversee the running of them. The Foundation Managers of the Middlehill School were Captain Carr Glyn, Canon Francis (or Frank) Huyshe, Mrs Paget and Mrs Lees. J. Guy and Mrs Sowter were the other two original managers.

The Church of St Michael was not the only prominent new building to have been erected in the village around the turn of the century. The Water Tower, with a capacity of 178,000 gallons, in Tower (or Turret) Lane, was built in 1903, by the Water Board of the Rural District Council, to supply the village, and remained a conspicuous landmark for 80 years, until it became redundant and was demolished.

When the Chapelry of St Michael and All Angels in the Parish of Wimborne Minster became an Ecclesiastical Parish in its own right, the Living, according to the Church Minute Book, was in the Patronage of "The Governors of the Possession, Revenues and Goods of the Free Grammar School of Queen Elizabeth in Wimborne Minster, County Dorset". The Patrons remain "The Corporation of Church Governors of Wimborne Minster". The Vicarage was built on a plot, given by the Bankes Estate, adjoining the Church.

The Church Hall or "Parish Room", as it was originally called, built at the expense of Mrs Lees and Mrs Paget, was erected in 1904. At the opening, 150 were entertained to "a substantial Tea", followed by a concert. The Church of England, like other denominations, marches on its stomach. The following month, a "Limelight Lantern Lecture" was given in the hall.

The 1903 edition of Kelly's Directory is the first to list Colehill as a separate place. It adheres, of course, to the rather oddly drawn parish boundaries of the time, and so we read the somewhat surprising information that "children of this parish attend the schools at Wimborne and Middle Hill, *Hampreston*".

John Cobb and Charles Coombes are listed as brickmakers, there are two blacksmiths, Joseph Guy and George Wilkins, and the wheelwright, James Wareham. Leigh Vineries is recorded, the owners then, and for several years afterwards, being E. Bourgaize and Co. Josiah Quertier moved up the hill from Leigh, to The Moorings, a house in Northleigh Lane, backing on to the Vineries, his home when the war began.

The Parish Magazine appeared first in November 1903. Apart from recording the exploits of the cricket and football clubs, it shed much light on other aspects of life in the village over the years. We learn, for example, that early in 1904, the last collection of mail "from the wall box" at Colehill Post Office was at 7.25 p.m. Spinning, as well as weaving, presumably as a cottage industry, continued as a local occupation, and Colehill tweeds seem to have been quite highly regarded, and indeed, enjoyed royal patronage. The Burrow's Wimborne Guide also mentions this industry. Referring to the local linen and cloth industry in the Middle Ages, it goes on: "A praiseworthy attempt to revive the manufacture of homespuns, and so give employment to the villagers, is being made in the neighbourhood, at Colehill."

The first advertisement appeared in the Church Magazine: "Nurse Bagshaw. Trained and Experienced Masseuse" and: "Mrs Blandford, Dress Maker & all kinds of needlework." A later advertisement offered cooking lessons "On Tuesdays to young ladies and to servants on Thursdays". Reference is made to what seems to have been a stormy meeting at Middlehill School, ending with some violence, during the General Election campaign in the spring of 1904.

The Church and School records remind us of the prevalence of infant mortality and of how rife sickness and disease were in that era, when the children of the less well-off were ill-clad and underfed. This was general throughout the country, of course, and not peculiar to Colehill. Epidemics of measles, mumps, chickenpox, diphtheria and influenza all caused the school to be closed for various periods during these years. Inadequate clothing and the poor state of the roads – none of these were made up at the time – resulted in low attendances during spells of inclement weather. There are frequent entries in the school "log" such as "Disastrously wet, 48 attended"; "Raining, 18 present" and "Steady downpour, 25 present". The nadir was reached one day in 1900, when, with a roll of 125 pupils, the attendance was nil, owing to rain and wind. Another handicap for the staff, the Headmistress and two assistants, and the children, was the lack of lighting. An entry in the "log" during 1905 records: "Too dark for reading."

In that same year, Rev Kindersley applied for a licence to keep 5 cwt. of calcium carbide. This may have been for domestic use also, but it was certainly primarily required for the Church, which then and for many years afterwards was lighted by acetylene gas.

It is amusing to note that the Vicar was lamenting, in the Magazine for January 1905: "We do not often get the old-fashioned Christmas Day of bright sunshine and a world clad in snow white"; he no doubt recalled childhood memories of the succession of severe winters around 1877 when the River Stour would be frozen over for several weeks at a time. In the same issue of the Magazine, a reference to the staffing of the school reflects the attitudes of a time long before "Women's Lib." – "... decided to have a Master at the head of the School instead of a Mistress. The School had grown so much of late that it was felt that it needed now a man's authority." F.M. Lodge was appointed and held the post for the next twenty years.

The Church ran a "Coal and Clothing Club" to help alleviate the lot of the poor; this was selling coal at 21 shillings a ton in 1907. The amenities of the village continued to increase. Milk was being delivered twice daily by a dairy in Little Lonnen. In 1908, one could hire a carriage or trap, and at Belle Vue, in Wimborne Road, a general stores was opened by H. Burling. The shop remained there for 70 years, but has now gone. Burling also advertised himself as a gardener, having been "A practical gardener for many years in gentlemen's places".

The Coffee Tavern was already fulfilling a number of functions: there was a miniature rifle range, among the recreational activities; it was the meeting place for the Parish Council, and the venue for Bible Classes, Sunday School and the church Mother's Meetings. The Cricket Club held its Committee and Annual General Meetings there from 1907. In 1908, it also started accommodating the School's cookery class for girls, and the following year, Charlie Matcham, short in stature and quite a "character" in the village, started a business there as a Cycle Agent and Repairer. He sold Ariel and Speedwell Cycles "from £6.10s.". His association with the Guy family was not limited to his business using their Coffee Tavern; he also lodged with "old" Joe and his wife, Elizabeth.

The Parish Magazine for March 1908 records the presentation of a flagpole and full-sized Union Jack to the School by Mrs Paget and her daughter, Adelaide – familiarly known locally as "Miss Addy". When the Flag was dedicated, the children saluted it and marched round it. The Vicar continues: "We hope it will tend to make the children learn to love the old flag and realise that they belong to a great Empire which is worthy of their loyal devotion."

Some progress was being made in the way of modern amenities. Although the Parish Council, whose members in the early years of the century included William Barrett, the retired baker and grocer, of Merrifield, Francis Devenish Guy, now at Colehill Farm, and Joseph Hardy Guy, still declined to provide street lighting, gas mains were laid along Wimborne Road, as far east as Northleigh Lane, in 1909, so that gas lighting was available for domestic purposes in that part of the village. In that same year, it was decided to *restrict* the opening hours at the Post Office to *8 a.m. to 8 p.m.*. On Wednesday, the early closing day, the premises were to close as early as 2 p.m. At Leigh, water pumped from wells was found to be unfit for drinking, but the water mains had been extended, by 1912, to supply much of the upper part of the village. In that year, the R.D.C. granted permission for the erection of telephone poles to Colehill and Leigh Vineries and a telephone call office was provided at the Post Office in 1913. The first Library in the village opened in 1913, organised by the Church, as the result of a bequest of some 200 books from Mrs Lees, who had recently died. Miss Henrietta Vaughan Williams, cousin of the composer, had come to live in the village and she was appointed Librarian.

The death of Mrs Lees caused the break-up of the Beaucroft Estate. Her sons-in-law sold off the upper part of the land, adjoining Wimborne Road, in plots of varying size. A large plot was bought by a man named Lamperd. There were changes, too, at North Leigh House, purchased by Louisa Ellis from the Glyns.

The new Primitive Methodist Chapel was built in 1913, the land being leased to the Trustees by the Bankes Estate for 99 years, at an annual rent of £1. William Habgood was the builder, and one of the foundation stones was laid by Joseph Hardy Guy – on behalf, according to the inscription, of his father, S. Guy. The cost of the building was £400, and a further charge of £3 was incurred for oil lamps. The new Chapel was opened in May, and Mrs Dorcas Habgood, daughter-in-law of the builder, played the harmonium outside the premises, accompanied by three fiddlers – perhaps borrowed from the Broomhill musicians – at the opening ceremony. The lease was, in fact, cancelled eight years later, when the land was sold to the Methodists. Among the names of the Trustees which appear both on the lease and the subsequent conveyance are Frank Wareham, a carpenter and brother of the wheelwright, Levi Dacombe and Reuben Hayward, a resident of Pilford Heath.

But, as the Methodists moved up the hill to their new church nearer the centre of the village, the war clouds were gathering, and perhaps it was not a coincidence that D.J. Cobb, advertising his boot and shoe shop in the village, in the Parish Magazine for April 1914, used a quotation from Kipling: "Boots, boots, boots."

COLEHILL ST. MICHAEL'S FOOTBALL CLUB, 1905–06. Seated, left to right Frank Barrett, G. Philpott, C. Coombs, Joe Guy (junior), Jack Bleathman, "Bossy" Cole, ?. On ground, left to right Jesse Hall, Tommy Cole. Standing, left to right F. Douch, "Farmer" J. Guy, Walt Richmond, Walt Habgood, F. Cole, E. Bleathman, Rev. C. E. Kindersley and Henry Habgood.

OPPOSITE

THE POST OFFICE and Smugglers Lane, looking down towards 'The Slop' and St. Michael's Church, circa 1908. The figure in the shop doorway is probably Frank Barrett, the postmaster, while the man holding the bicycle has been "positively" identified as a Mr. Newman, a Mr. Wareham and a Mr. Willis!

SMUGGLERS LANE, circa 1905, looking from the Church crossroads towards the Post Office corner. The dip in the road was known locally as "The Slop". The woman in the foreground is Mrs. Ann Parfitt — "Granny Bloomer".

ROWLANDS, circa 1910, with the entrance to Glen House on the left.

WILLIAM HABGOOD'S WORKMEN engaged in the erection of the "new" Methodist Church, 1913.

THE GUY FAMILY, about 1910. Mr. and Mrs. Francis Devenish, seated, with Ted (great-grandson) between, and, standing, Joseph Hardy (son), on left, and Frank (grandson).

THE STOTE FAMILY, circa 1914, in their 1910 Talbot. Arthur, who became Vicar of Colehill in 1918 and who changed his name by Deed Poll to Stote-Blandy in 1934, is at the wheel, with his wife beside him, with their daughter, Frances, on her lap. The other child is their daughter, Marjorie, and the lady standing beside the car is Stote's mother-in-law, 'Granny' Blandy.

EMMA HABGOOD'S LAUNDRY (now Colehill Service Station) at the junction of Wimborne Road and Leigh Lane (now Kyrchil Way) in about 1916. Emma (or Emily) Habgood is second from the right, with her daughter, Ethel, on her left.

Chapter 7

THE GREAT WAR AND THE TWENTIES

It is difficult to gauge the impact upon Colehill of the Great War of 1914-18. The young men of the village went away to the war: it is not easy to say how many, a couple of hundred, perhaps. Thirty-six did not come back. The War Memorial stands at the intersection known as the Fiveways, commemorating those killed in battle. The names are there for all to read and they testify to the tragic impact on many of the village families.

The Wayside Cross, as the War Memorial was originally termed, standing on a mound made up of many cartloads of broken pots from Leigh Vineries, was dedicated on 5 June 1920. Within the Cross is a cavity, into which was cemented a small bottle "containing a record written on parchment cut from an ancient deed".

A memorial plaque in St Michael's Church records the death of Arthur Lonsdale, of The Further House. The wooden cross marking his grave at the battlefield of Neuve Chapelle in France was returned to his mother several years after the war and stands within the church.

The Vicar, writing in the Parish Magazine in August 1914, before scarcely a shot had been fired in anger, prophesied with uncanny accuracy: "Our country is engaged in the greatest conflict ever known."

The outbreak of war coincided with a local crisis of some dimensions, the Middlehill School being in need of large and costly alterations following the report of Government inspectors. The sum of £250 would have to be raised by subscription to meet the expected bill. The School would be enlarged, classrooms would be separated, and improvements made to heating, lighting and ventilation. Most of the work was completed during the school summer holidays.

One of the scholars has recalled the great ceremonial of Fridays at Middlehill in that era. This was the day when Captain Carr Glyn, a School Manager, arrived in his horse-drawn carriage for his weekly visit. Another remembers being instructed to curtsy to the great ladies of the village, and in order to avoid doing so, hiding in a hedge, on the approach of Mrs Georgiana Paget, being wheeled in her Bath-chair by her handyman, George Humphries.

Three men from the Church Choir were among the first to enlist in the Army, in the fervour of patriotism which gripped the country on the outbreak of war. The Vicar, in the Magazine for September 1914, mentions a letter received from one of the three, which heartily recommends the soldier's life at Aldershot. The names of twenty Colehill men who had joined up, mainly in the Army, with a couple in both the Navy and the Marines, are given in the October Magazine. The well-known village names already referred to are well represented in the list. Stanley Clarke enlisted in the 5th Dorsets, later transferred to the Royal Flying Corps, and was awarded the Military Cross. As early as April 1915, the first fatal casualties were recorded. Thereafter, scarcely one issue of the Magazine appeared without further names of those killed in action.

Beaucroft House, Mrs Lees's home before her death, had been converted into a Red Cross Hospital by the early months of 1917 to help deal with the wounded from the Front. Miss Carr Glyn was the Commandant, and soldiers in their "Hospital Blue" were a familiar sight.

The girls at the School busied themselves with "comforts for the troops", knitting socks and mufflers, and the School "log" for 1917 recorded an entry that the children were gathering acorns "for use at the Holton Heath Cordite Works". The connection between the fruit of the oak tree and a lethal explosive is difficult to establish, but it seems that the acorns were ground down to become a constituent of gunpowder. There was an appeal in the Parish Magazine for "fruit stones and hard nutshells for the manufacture of anti-Gas Masks". The civil population was exhorted to cultivate all gardens and every available plot of land, to produce more home-grown food. A potato sprayer was purchased by the Council in 1918, to be used by the parishioners free of charge. The threat of starvation seems to have been very real. At the behest of the Bishop, Rev Cyril Kindersley spent six months away working on a farm at Winterborne Kingston, wielding, perhaps, a pitchfork, instead of his more familiar cricket bat. Returning in October 1917, he shortly afterwards resigned the living and offered his services to the Church Army, at the Front.

He was succeeded as Vicar at the beginning of 1918 by Arthur Stote (who, adding his wife's name to his own, took the name Stote-Blandy in 1934). Arthur Stote was an enthusiastic local historian, and the pages of the Parish Magazine were enlivened from time to time, over the next few years, by the results of his researches; he was also a stickler for insisting on the correct pronunciation of the name of the village. Another of his interests was painting, and he produced several pictures of local scenes.

The first ecumenical move on Colehill was the planned open-air service on the fourth anniversary of the outbreak of war. This joint venture by St Michael's and the Primitive Methodists was, alas, abandoned because of bad weather, just as the harmonium was about to be taken to the chosen venue, at the Post Office corner.

The news of the Armistice on 11 November 1918 reached Frank Barrett, the Postmaster, shortly before 11.30 a.m., and he hastened to the Vicarage with the good tidings. By 11.45, the bells of the Church were being rung, to announce to the village that the war was over. This was followed by an impromptu Service of Thanksgiving.

There seems to have been some dispute soon after the war as to the ownership of the Parish Hall. Whether the title deeds vested the property in the name of the village or that of the Church was settled, it seems, simply by appealing to the former Vicar, Cyril Kindersley, who pronounced "that the Hall was *not* public property, but belonged to the Benifice".

The Primitive Methodists, in their new Chapel in Lonnen Road, had no resident minister, but were served by visiting preachers, and flourished down the years with strong support from the local congregation, among whom the Moody and Habgood families were prominent. The oil lamps gave way to gas lighting in due course, and the fragmentation of the Methodists was healed by the Act of Union, which united the Wesleyans, the Primitives and the old "United" Methodists in one organisation in 1932.

The String Band was still performing at the end of the war, and for many years afterwards, surviving, in fact, another war, until the late 1940s. Joseph Hardy Guy, who had taken over Colehill Farm, died in 1921 at the age of 66, and his nephew, Alfred Dacombe, who played the violin, became the leader of the band in the early 'twenties, when it was in its heyday. Among the players around this time were four Habgoods, three Dacombes, including Alfred's daughter, Frances, and three Guys – Joseph Hardy Guy, until his death, his son, Joseph Edward, and his great-grandson, another Joseph.

Colehill seems to have enjoyed the talents of a number of musicians at that period; there was a String Quartette, consisting of two Habgoods, a Dacombe and Frank Barrett, the Postmaster and baker; there was a Colehill "Regimental" Jazz Band, and some years afterwards, there is reference to Mr Hallett's Orchestra. There was a duo, the violinist Alfred Dacombe and Reg Welch, on the piano, sometimes augmented as a trio, which played at dances. These men seem to have been endowed with immense energy: the story is told of Alfred Dacombe, a plasterer by trade, that he would cycle to Crichel House, do a day's work there, wash and change, then cycle, with his violin on his back, the thirty miles or so to play at a dance at Weymouth, and then, in the small hours, cycle the thirty miles back, to start another day's work, at 7 a.m., at Crichel. Welch was also a member of the String Orchestra, and later became its conductor. Apart from Church and School Choirs, there was a sixty-strong Colehill Choral Society. There was, too, at a later date, a Boy Scouts band.

A branch of the Women's Institute was formed in the village at the start of 1919, largely on the initiative of Henrietta (or Rita) Vaughan Williams, who was its first Secretary, but who died in 1921, at the age of 45. The President was Mrs Senior. The WI was campaigning –

without success – within a year of its formation for the removal of refuse heaps in the village and for a refuse collection from the houses. There was also, for many years in the 'twenties and 'thirties, an active Men's Institute, and the familiar village names, Farrant, Barrett, Guy and Habgood are prominent among the officers and committeemen.

Among members of the Parish Council, after the war, were George Solly, who had been Chairman since 1902, until he resigned shortly before his death, Rev Arthur Stote, Frank Barrett, and Joseph Edward Guy. The first signs of animosity between the Colehill Parish Council and the Wimborne Urban District Council seems to stem from an incident in 1922, when some employees of the Wimborne Council are alleged to have forced their way into a store at their offices, in which the Colehill Council kept their parish records, and to have then thrown these documents into the adjoining garden.

The Cricket Club (which had lain dormant during the Great War and was not revived until another four years had elapsed after the Armistice) and the Football Club, which had restarted much sooner, seem to have had varied fortunes during the next few years.

A meeting in February 1923 decided to re-form the Cricket Club. The Men's Institute, under the "umbrella" of the Church, was no longer able to help subsidise the cricketers as it had before the war, and the club would, in future, have to stand on its own feet financially. Thus, the decision was taken to drop the "St Michaels" from the name and the club was revived as, simply, the Colehill Cricket Club. With the permission of the owner, and the tenant, Johnny Coakes, who lived and farmed at Deans Grove, the Club played on "Mr Solly's field", their present home, but at that time, in the grounds of Bells House. Frank Barrett, Charles Hay, the younger Joe Guy and Henry Habgood continued their association from the pre-war Club and George Bannister was the new President.

Whether the revival was as brief as the records suggest is not certain, but nothing appears in the Club Minutes between April 1924 and the A.G.M. of 1928. Hay, as President, Barrett, Joe Guy, and Henry Habgood remain from the "Old Guard" and Joe Guy's son, Archie, who was to render the club such splendid service in various capacities over the next 37 years and who is commemorated by a wrought-iron gate at the ground, was the captain.

Solly died within a couple of years of the revival of the Cricket Club, but his widow sanctioned the continued use of her field by the Club. Cattle grazed on the ground between matches and the next major landmark in the Club's history was the fencing off of the "square" throughout the year, with the permission of Coakes, the tenant farmer.

A harmonious relationship existed between the Cricket and Football Clubs – J. Richmond was secretary of both at one time and Barrett served both Clubs as treasurer in the early 'twenties. The footballers also moved their home, and now played on the field behind the Coffee Tavern in Colehill Lane. They had changed their colours to those of the County – green and white quartered shirts – and they changed in the Tavern where "old" Mrs Guy – Elizabeth – boiled water for their baths. At a later date, they moved on down the hill and crossed the road to play at the field called "Patey's", taking its name from its owner of thirty years before, Thomas Patey. Bert Cole, who had a herd of dairy cattle at Long Lane, grazed the animals on this field, but permitted the footballers to build a hut there, to serve as a changing room.

Among their opponents in the season of 1920-21, in the Second Division of the Dorset League, were Poole Hornets, Poole Congregationalists, Poole Comrades, Wessex Aircraft, 2nd Battalion Tank Corps Bovington, Wimborne Town and a team from Bourne valley, which was the industrial sector of Bournemouth and Poole, called, simply, "Gas Works". Two rather curious entries appear in their accounts for that season – the purchase of "Amusement Tax Stamps" and an item for violin strings; the footballers, too, is seems, added to the music of the village.

The Club was still called "Colehill St Michael's", and

perhaps significantly, Rev Arthur Stote, the Vicar, was on the committee. Archie Guy, Walter Cole (cousin of Bert), Reg Welch and David Bryant were among the players; Henry Farrant and Henry Habgood were both linesmen and these two, together with Joe Guy, also served on the committee. The Club continued playing during the 'twenties and 'thirties, but seems to have been dissolved on the outbreak of the second war.

A branch of the County Free Library, under the Carnegie Trust, independent of the Church Library, was opened in the village in the autumn of 1922.

Georgiana Paget died in February 1919, at the age of 97. She was the widow of the Colonel who had been so instrumental in founding the local church, mother of "Miss Addy" and of Brigadier-General Wellesley Paget, a veteran of the South African War, when he led "Paget's Horse", and of the Great War, when he had commanded an artillery division before being invalided home; these she had outlived, and there were seven other sons. She had played a prominent role in village affairs, being not only the first Churchwarden, but also an original Trustee and Foundation Manager of Middlehill School.

The population of Colehill, through the years, seems to have included many who lived to a great age. Ann Parfitt died in 1920, three months short of her 97th birthday. She lived at Merrifield and seems to have been quite a "character" in the village. She was familiarly known, on account of an item of her costume, as "Granny Bloomer", and invariably carried a long forked stick, which she is said to have used to administer summary justice on any misbehaving child. Her diet was said to have regularly included a slice of bread and butter, thickly spread with mustard. She had been a widow since 1860 and had had to labour in the fields from morning to night for tenpence a day. 116 living descendants, including a great-great-granddaughter, survived her. She had been recorded in the Census as far back as 1861, when she was living in Long Lane. John Hatchard, the first Churchwarden of Colehill (together with Mrs Paget) died in 1922, at the age of 79. He had been keenly interested in local church affairs long before the erection of the present building, in 1893.

Early in 1925, the death is recorded of a resident of Pilford, Stephen Burden, father of 21 children, "the oldest inhabitant, at least 93". One of his sons, Edward, a Church-warden at St Michael's, was a a smallholder at Pilford Heath: he was, according to his daughter-in-law, passionately fond of bananas, and kept a secret hoard of the fruit. Edward's son, Alfred, gamekeeper to Colonel O'Kelly, who rented Uddens House from Mrs Oldfield, married Frances Dacombe, one of the violinists in the String Orchestra. An octogenarian herself, she has retained vivid memories of the village in the 'twenties.

Elizabeth Frances Osman, needlewoman and seamstress at Canford School, is remembered as another of the "characters" of the village, walking every day to Wimborne and back to buy meat for her cats. Several years ago, in the spring of 1971, the author interrupted her busily *chopping wood* outside her thatched cottage, Mount Pleasant. She was, at that time, the oldest *native* living on Colehill, and looking forward to her 93rd birthday the following July. She predicted that the cottage, 200 years old, in which her grandmother had lived, and owned by the Bankes Estate, would be demolished on her own death. And so it was, a few years later.

The Kelly's Directory for 1920 introduces one or two new names to the village. Mackay and Wills are given as fruit growers at Leigh Vineries, with Captain Frank Mackay occupying Leigh Vineries House. This partnership, which had bought the business from Bourgaize and Co., did not survive very long, A.R. Wills breaking away to set up his own business in Hampshire. Mackay's next partner was Murray, and Mackay and Murray grew tomatoes, cucumbers and "large quantities" of grapes.

Oliver's Farm, in Middle Hill, is mentioned in the 1920 directory, and presumably stood near Oliver's House. The farm is given as the address of George Smith, farm bailiff to Mrs Oldfield, owner of the Uddens Estate. Perhaps this was the same George Smith recorded as a "higgler" in a directory 35 years previously. Other farms are mentioned, but not Park Homer Farm. Long Lane Farm was occupied by William Oakley Burgess. Jimmy Wareham was still the wheelwright and Joseph Edward Guy is described as "blacksmith, cycle agent and engineer". Joe, footballer, cricketer and musician, had succeeded his father, Joseph Hardy Guy, as the village blacksmith, and was the last in the line going back several generations which had owned the family business. When he died, during the war of 1939-45, the smithy closed down. His elder son – also named Joseph Edward – was killed in the earlier war, but another son, the cricketing Archie, was to carry the family name on, with much distinction, for another generation.

Beaucroft House, following its use as a hospital during the war, became the home of a retired Royal Navy Captain, George Steer, an appropriate name for a sailor; apt, too, in another sense of the word, as he also farmed there, until his death in 1928. He was succeeded, oddly enough, by another man bearing a name with farming associations, Bullock. Steer's wife, Agnes, was the owner of the Dairy Cottage, on the opposite side of Beaucroft Lane, in her own right, until it was sold in 1926. The upper part of the Beaucroft Estate had been sold off following the death of Mrs Lees before the war, but the remainder still occupied a considerable area, 32 acres in extent, from Beaucroft Lane to Northleigh Lane.

Meanwhile the land to the west of Beaucroft Lane, beyond the Dairy Cottage, had been sold by Coakes to Leonard Sims, a builder and surveyor turned farmer, who clearly realised its potential for residential development.

Mrs Berrington became the new incumbent of Park Homer House, on the death of Mrs Paget, and quickly distinguished herself by closing the public footpath adjoining her property, which had been a right of way for at least forty years, at "Park Homer Carriage Entrance". She eventually agreed to a compromise, where the footpath would still run across her land, but be diverted from her Carriage Drive, and run alongside it, thus removing the peasants from her immediate gaze.

This was not the only instance of landowners obstructing rights of way across their estates. A bridle-track across Cannon Hill was obstructed in 1925 by a gate, erected by Mrs Oldfield. She it was, too, who disputed a path from Middle Hill to Pilford Heath, which had been a right of way for more than fifty years, closed it and diverted it; and moreover, was successful in having the diversion officially sanctioned, neither the Parish Council nor the Rural District Council being prepared to bring a lawsuit against her. Part of the Cannon Hill Plantation was sold to the Forestry Commission in the late 'twenties, and we find that body very quickly similarly engaged: both a footpath and a bridleway were stopped, just below "Cannon Hill Clump" in 1928.

Another of the rather "grand" ladies of the village, Mrs Farrer, arrived in the late 'twenties, to take up residence at Park Homer.

A note in the Church Magazine for December 1923 recorded that "the Acetylene Apparatus in the Hall is practically worn out" and there is a suggestion that both the Church and the Hall might be lighted by electricity if the Bournemouth Company start to operate in Wimborne. No hasty decision was taken on this matter; and indeed, not until the early months of 1926 was the issue resolved. It was decided to light the Church, the Hall and the Vicarage by gas, there being "excellent reasons against electric light, acetylene or petrol plants".

The Wimborne Gas Company had got as far as the Post Office with its pipe-laying by September 1926, and eventually, the gas lighting was installed in the Church before Christmas. The Vicar recorded the following conversation overheard locally, in which coal gas seems to have been confused with incense:

"I 'ear they're getting very 'igh at Colehill Church."

"Oh! How's that?"

"Well, they've put gas into the Church."

From 1922, the village boys over the age of eleven went to school at Wimborne, no longer attending Middlehill. H.E.V. Griffith, "a young man of energetic personality", was appointed Headmaster of Middlehill School in March 1925, in succession to Lodge. The school "log" mentions that the Headmaster and boys extinguished heath fires at Cannon Hill in both 1927 and 1928.

The Girl Guides seem to have appeared on the scene in Colehill earlier, by more than a year, than the Boy Scouts, a patrol, or company, having been started by "Jimmy" Hewett and Mabel Digby in September 1924, and officially registered in the autumn of 1925. The meeting place was the Parish Hall. Miss Hewett, familiarly known as "Jimmy" from childhood and seldom by her Christian name of Margaret, remained actively involved with the Colehill Guides for half a century. She was Captain of the Company until 1960, and continued to serve on the committee afterwards, becoming President of the local Association. She was also active in other village affairs, and was, for many years, the Secretary of St Michael's Church. Miss Digby was succeeded as Lieutenant by Irene Smart, who became the Captain when Miss Hewett resigned. There was, too, a Brownie Pack, run by the Vicar's daughter, Frances Stote-Blandy.

A separate Girl Guide Company and Brownie Pack was started at the Melverley School six or seven years later. Miss Reid was Captain of the Guides and Miss Moldram was in charge of the Brownies.

The original minute book of the Colehill Scouts records an inaugural meeting of the committee, at the Vicarage, on 20 March 1926. Those present included Sir James Brooks, Rev Arthur Stote, Joe Guy, Mr Griffith – his name is occasionally spelt with a final "s" in these records – Mabel Digby, and her sister, Edith, with A.C. Matthews in the Chair. Mabel Digby was both Secretary and Treasurer, with Edith as her Assistant. The "energetic" Griffith was the Scoutmaster.

Subsequent meetings were held at Highwood, the Digby home. An effort seems to have been made to persuade Father Doody, presumably the local Roman Catholic priest, to join the Scouts Committee, perhaps with a view to giving the movement a broader based Christian support, but this, apparently, did not materialise. In May 1926, eighteen boys were reported to be "keen scouts". It was decided to defer starting a Cub Pack, although in November, the Troop numbered thirty-seven – twenty-three scouts, six rovers and eight cubs. A Scout band was started, to add to the music of the village, and a photograph around this time shows this to have consisted of three drummers and at least four buglers.

The Scoutmaster also found time to be the conductor of both the School and WI Choirs, and to be active in church affairs. It seems probable that he was, too, the same "Griffith" who umpired for the Colehill Cricket Club – a man of many parts. However, his reign was fairly brief, and he moved from the district in 1929, his successor as headmaster of the School being appointed in the summer of that year. Although the Guides continued to flourish under Miss Hewett, the Scouts, left without a leader, became dormant. Apparently, no successor to Griffith could be found and more than nineteen years elapsed before there was a Colehill Scout Troop again.

George Langer, who succeeded Solly as Chairman of the Parish Council, was remarking, as early as 1926, "how of late years the parish had changed from purely rural to semi-urban".

But many of the modern amenities were still lacking. Highwood, opposite the Church, was the first house on Colehill to be supplied with electricity, produced from its own private generator. Beaucroft and North Leigh were other houses with their own generators. Highwood was the home of the Digby family; Reginald, an Oxford Cricket "Blue", was a member of an Irish aristocratic family, self-exiled following the "Troubles" there during the war; he had died in 1927, but his daughters remained active in village affairs. Mabel was involved in the Guide movement and in the Women's Institute, became a Parish Councillor, and together with Frank Barrett, started the Choral Society; Edith was the librarian in the village, and belonged to the local branch of the League of Nations Union; and both sisters did much charitable work for the deprived children of the East End of London.

The staff of Highwood included Clara Smart, George Wall, Harry Cuff, Walter Cole and his future wife, Gladys Thomas. Mrs Smart, who was related to the farmer, Johnny Coakes, was cook and housekeeper to the Digbys, having earlier served Sir John Elliott Lees and his family at Lytchett Manor as "Under Nurse". Her daughter, Irene, grew up to be prominent in village affairs of a later era, especially in connection with the Church and the Girl Guide Company, and finished her teaching career as Deputy Head of Middlehill School.

Wall was the chauffeur, in succession to a chauffeuse, Biddy Ramsbottom, Cuff succeeded Burt as gardener and Walter Cole worked at Highwood as a "garden boy" before following the family tradition and going into the bricklaying trade. His grandfather had helped build the Parish Room in the early years of the century. His grandmother, Elizabeth Parfitt before marriage, was a laundrywoman, in Lonnen Road, before the war, Mrs Paget being among her customers, and his mother continued in the family tradition of laundresses, including the Hanhams among her customers. Ann Parfitt – "Granny Bloomer" – was a great-aunt. The names of two of Walter's cousins – Percy and Reginald – are among those on the War Memorial. Walter's brother, William, survived the war, but with a bullet in his body to remind him of those grim years, and has lived into his nineties. Walter, the youngest of the family, was only five years old when the war began. He lived to be eighty-one and was blessed with an excellent memory. His anecdotes and reminiscences of his boyhood and youth conjured up a vivid picture of Colehill in the twenties.

His wife, Gladys, was the sister of Reg Thomas, the cheerful milk roundsman, who will be remembered by many still living in the village. She was in the service, before moving to the Digby household, of the Stringers, who moved to North Leigh House in 1921. Northleigh Lane separated the House, somewhat unusually, from its coach house and the quarters of the outdoor servants. The Coach House, now converted into a spacious private dwelling and commanding a high price in the housing market, and the cottages occupied by the chauffeur and the head gardener, converted into a single dwelling house, now known as Northleigh Lodge, but called, earlier, Holly Lodge, still stand. The kitchen gardens of the house adjoined, also on the eastern side of the lane, and further up the hill. The original lodges to North Leigh (which it seems to have become fashionable at this time to spell as two words) stood one on each side of the drive to the house itself.

Mrs Louisa Ellis sold the North Leigh Estate in 1921 to Selwyn Stringer. Stringer, an industrialist from Birmingham, died in 1959, and the family left the area within the next couple of years. The estate covered more than eighteen acres when purchased by Stringer, including not only the house and its grounds, but an area on the eastern side of Northleigh Lane running from a plantation abutting on to Kyrchil Lane, beyond Rowney House, at the top, to halfway down the hill, and including the coach house and cottages, and the fields on each side of them. After Stringer's death, the estate was sold off in small parcels: houses now stand on the site of the Plantation, but the scene in Northleigh Lane remains very much the same, retaining its pastoral appearance. The house and its gardens fell into disrepair, and were only rescued when they were purchased in 1966 by Stanley and Margaret Walker. Although belonging to Colehill's present rather than past, the Walkers' efforts to restore the house and its grounds to their former glory must be recorded, as must their preservation of old documents, photographs and other memorabilia of the Stringer era, which have come into their hands. These and the splendid restoration of the dining and drawing rooms, the billiards room, the butler's pantry, the hall and the staircase conjure up an age of considerable elegance and gracious living, perhaps equalling the opulence of the great days of the Webbs, with dinner parties, dances, tennis parties and so on, throughout the two decades which separated the wars. The ashes of Stringer's former chauffeur, Gates, were scattered in the grounds of the house.

Rowney House, at the top of Northleigh Lane, became the home of Charlie Hay after the war. Two brothers were employed by him, Percy Wayman, as gardener, and Fred, originally his coachman, and later the chauffeur for his Fiat. Hay, himself, never drove. The garage, previously the coach-house, has survived the demolition of the house and still stands, itself converted into a private dwelling many years ago.

The Digbys were believed to have been the first Colehill family to own a motor car, a Buick. Motor vehicles were a familiar sight in the village by that time; indeed, Henry Farrant, a baker at Leigh Common before the war, started a carrier's business in Colehill, with a Ford lorry, when he returned to civilian life. The corrugated iron garage for his Ford still stands, a short distance back from the roadside in Wimborne Road, opposite the Beaucroft School. This is now the property of Mrs Grace Nisbet, who lives in one of the 400-year-old cottages behind the building. She has been kind enough to allow me to examine the deeds of the property. These encapsulate much of the history of the area in the past 150 years, and reveal that the plot of land on which her present property stands was once much larger, extending along Wimborne Road as far as Beaucroft Lane. Indeed, the records show that the extent was at one time even greater, embracing the whole area, amounting to six acres, at the top of the hill, from Northleigh Lane to Beaucroft Lane, part of the old Beaucroft Estate.

John Lamperd, a retired coal merchant, who had purchased the land, sold part of it to William Joseph Habgood; Habgood sold his plot to Henry Farrant, and eventually it became the property of the Nisbets. The adjoining plot, extending to the Fiveways junction, was split into two. Lamperd sold the more easterly of the two, the Beechwood site, to John Quertier in 1915. The other, which included the old Pleasure House Plantation, changed hands in 1919, when it was bought by the bootmaker, David Cobb and his wife, Amelia. Cobb, grandson of the founder of the brickworks, was survived by his wife, and the property was later inherited by *their* son, David Cobb, junior, the chiropodist-cum-hairdresser. These old documents also suggest that Wimborne Road was, at one time, known as Church Road, presumably remembering the old Iron Church which stood there more than a century ago. "Church Road" also appears in other records of that era.

Elizabeth Oldfield must have been one of the first women motorists in the district. She is remembered by many of the older villagers as a somewhat accident-prone and aggressive driver, driving imperiously on the crown of the road, with a tendency to clear pedestrians out of her way along the narrow, unmade tracks of the time with a blaring horn. On one occasion, when visiting the Digbys, she made a spectacular arrival at Highwood, depositing her car upside down in the garden pond.

Speeding motorists were causing anxiety as far back as 1928. The Council Minutes record complaints of excessive speed by motor vehicles on the village roads "To be brought to the notice of the Police Superintendent", at a time when Lonnen Road, Colehill Lane, and many other roads remained no more than gravel tracks. The Automobile Association were to be approached with a view to the erection of a warning notice near the Post Office.

The main thoroughfare through the village, Wimborne Road and Middlehill Road, was surfaced with coal tar in the late 'twenties; this followed complaints about the state of the "main road". But most of the roads still had a gravel surface, and lacked footpaths, until the early 1930s, and even later in some cases. The roads were "officially" named, the names that we are familiar with today, except that Northleigh Lane was originally to be called "Northleigh Road" and Middlehill Road changed its name at the School, in those days, to Canford Bottom, and the roads were adorned with name-plates for the first time in 1930. An objection was raised to the close proximity to the War Memorial of the sign indicating the start of Colehill Lane and so it was removed. The Bankes Estate refused permission for its erection on the opposite side of the road, and this stretch of the highway remained apparently incognito, and still does so, more than sixty years later.

Direction posts were erected at the junction of "Ringwood Road" and "Northleigh Road" and at the foot of "Church Hill" at its junction with Long Lane. The widening of Wimborne Road, between Cobbs Road and Beaucroft Lane, was canvassed. Giddy Lake, which remains an unmade road sixty years later, was the cause of some anxiety in 1930, with flood water running down the hill from a spring at the top, in rainy weather. There were complaints about damage to roads caused by motor lorries hauling gravel from the pit between Middle Hill School and Pilford Heath.

The first motor bus service, on Saturdays only, began about 1926, to be augmented later by the Poole and District Company's service on Tuesdays. The Hants and Dorset Company started running a service in 1930. Pneumatic tyres had come into use about three years previously, but early bus travel, and indeed, any journeys by motor vehicle in the early 'twenties, must have been extremely uncomfortable, in the age of unmade roads, solid tyres and rudimentary springing.

There was considerable competition for traffic on the route from Wimborne to Bournemouth, running along Leigh Road, between the Hants and Dorset Company and a new firm, the Imperial, which started operating in 1929. This led not only to some furious driving, which resulted in one Hants and Dorset bus finishing up in Leigh Pond, but also to a "price war". In April 1930, the Hants and Dorset cut the cost of a *return* ticket from Wimborne to Bournemouth to *sixpence* – there were, of course, 240 pence to the pound in those days. The Imperial was beaten, and sold out the following month.

Motor vehicles, then, were quite common in and around Colehill by 1930. But old ways die hard, and Mrs Truell, of Onslow, was still to be seen, always dressed in mauve, being driven through the village, in her horse-drawn carriage. The Hatchards, at Highlands, employed a coachman, to drive the family horse-drawn carriage.

At Bells, the Solly family later kept horses only for riding, and these were still stabled in part of the old coach house, the remainder of which became a garage for the family car. A chauffeur was employed, whose daughter, Olive Way, later Mrs Butler, could remember, from childhood, her family living in the upper storey of the coach house. Her mother was a parlourmaid at Bells House. The old coach house has been converted into a substantial private dwelling. Three sisters, Bertha, Jessie and Rosa Damen, were among the Sollys' staff of servants. Bertha was a nursemaid and Rosa was a housemaid.

Every Tuesday, there would be the spectacle of herds of cattle and flocks of sheep being driven over the hill, down to Rowlands and St John's, on their way to the Wimborne Market. The great houses, and those slightly less grand, dominated the scene, together with the humbler cottages. The Pilford section of Lonnen Road, beyond Sandy Lane, became a residential district. The top of the hill was still largely tree-clad, although a group of very tall pine trees was felled when the gas-lit Council houses at Glynville were built.

Perhaps these pines were the trees lamented in a poem of 1929:

> "Now nothing of that fragrant wood remains.
> Her very pines
> Were, dying, borne away
> To prop unlovely pits
> Beyond the day."

These lines, part of a poem called "Resurgam" by its author, appeared under the title "Colehill, 1929", when published. They were written by Frances Bliss, a remarkable woman, who lived, later as something of a recluse, in Leigh Lane, to a great age. Her elder sister was the Principal of the Melverley Girls' School, at the top of Rowlands.

Laundering, for the well-to-do of the village, and indeed, from further afield, seems to have become very much a "cottage industry" for the womenfolk. Elizabeth Cole (née Parfitt) has already been noted as one laundress and she was one of several following this occupation in the village in the nineteenth century; among others of later generations was Emma Habgood. She employed a small staff at her wash-house on the site of the present garage premises in Wimborne Road. She used to dry her washing on the bushes across the road, on the site of the old Iron Church, and the scent of the pine trees was supposed to have enhanced the finished product. She collected and delivered the laundry by donkey-cart; a schoolgirl of that time remembered the sad end of the donkey, which finally came to rest one day at the top of Rowlands. Mrs Elsworth, not far away, in Cobbs Road, was another noted laundry-woman. Mrs Thompson did the washing for the Solly family, and another Mrs Habgood, Clara Habgood, at Pilford, was laundrywoman for Mrs Oldfield, of Uddens. Edward Burden's wife followed the same occupation, her principal customer being the Wimborne doctor, Kaye le Fleming. Lydia Cobb, in Lonnen Road, was another washerwoman; in Smugglers Lane, Mary Short was laundress for the Digbys, and dried her washing among the trees opposite, in the "Triangle". She lived in one of a pair of cottages near the Post Office, afterwards converted into a single dwelling. Her next-door neighbour, Miss Fidler, was a pigeon-fancier.

Another of the "cottage industries" involving the women of the village was glove-making. These were knitted string gloves for horse riders. The string was delivered by a Blandford firm, who later collected the finished product, payment being at the rate of ninepence per pair of men's gloves, so twenty-seven pairs had to be knitted to earn these women one pound. Gloves for women and children were paid for at the reduced rate of sixpence and fourpence-halfpenny per pair respectively.

The 1928 Ordnance Survey map shows several properties along the southern side of Wimborne Road, with the other side partly wooded and the rest still open country. There was a scattering of cottages in Colehill Lane, the upper part of Lonnen Road and in Sandy Lane. The gravel pits, owned by Mrs Oldfield, are shown, roughly on the area now occupied by Brackenhill Road – these were still being worked at this time. Squibb, a gravel merchant from Holtwood, using a horse and cart, worked these pits some years previously, and a new quarry at Pilford Heath had been opened during the war. Damen, the Agent for the Uddens Estate, was complaining, in 1920, that Middlehill School children were throwing down guard fencing to the pits.

"Elliott's Grave" is marked, on the 1928 map, approximating to the position now occupied by the shops in Middlehill Road. The house and extensive outbuildings of Park Homer connected with Middlehill Road via a lengthy drive, emerging opposite the School, with Olivers House standing at this junction.

The reservoir, presumably supplying Leigh Vineries, is shown, where it remained until a few years ago, when Vineries Close was built on the site. The area between Beaucroft and North Leigh House is shown as woodland, traversed by a multitude of footpaths. Lady Marjorie Balfour, elder daughter of Sir Charles Rugge-Price, lived at Beaucroft House for many years, and she has recalled a path through the woods, giving access from the house to Northleigh Lane.

Both brickworks had long since disappeared, with Cobb's old site now being used as a farm, known appropriately as Brickyard Farm, leased by Frampton, and later, Peckham, from the Bankes Estate.

OPPOSITE

MIDDLEHILL SCHOOL Class 1 of about 1920. Seated, left to right are Albert Palmer, Fred Richmond, Leonard Baker, Frank Guest, Tom Richmond, Charlie Bullen, Eddie Morton. Standing, front row of girls, left to right, ?, Rosie Christopher, Vera Richmond, ?, Ethel Newman, Eva Cole. Second row, left to right, Beryl Shiner, Ethel Shearing, Frances Richmond, Winnie Richmond, Marjorie Cullen, Winnie Hellier, Dorothy Moody, F. M. Lodge (headmaster). Back row, left to right Cyril Hall, ?, Charlie Sawtell, Leslie Cullen, Edgar Habgood and Walter Cole.

MIDDLEHILL SCHOOL, circa 1920.

OPPOSITE
MIDDLEHILL SCHOOL Class 2, in about 1920. Front row, left to right Shearing, George Cox, Winston King, Bill Hayward, Willie Moody, Ken Hall, Frank Richmond. Middle row, left to right, Lily Frampton, Mary Cox, Lois Hayward, Elsie Burden, Lily Christopher, Winnie Newman, Beattie Shearing. Back row, left to right Gwen Gumbleton, Roy Mitchell, George Shearing, Bill Sawtell, Billy Moore, Ivy Hellier and F. M. Lodge (headmaster).

OPPOSITE, bottom
COLEHILL REGIMENTAL JAZZ BAND, about 1922. In the front row, second from the left is Albert Cole, and third from the right is Vic Bailey. The drummer is George Dacombe.

FRANK BARRETT, driving his bakers' van, circa 1922.

ST. MICHAEL'S CHURCH, from an original painting, dated 1923.

CROQUET ON THE LAWN OF HIGHWOOD, in about 1922.

COLEHILL ST. MICHAEL'S FOOTBALL CLUB, 1924-25 (photographed at Cuthbury, Wimborne). Seated, left to right Frampton, George Habgood, Howard Rogers, Vic Hall, last man unknown. Standing (middle row) left to right, Bert Guy, Bill Honeybun, Tom Gomm, Archie Guy, Percy Wareham, William Bellinger, Frank Barrett. Standing (back row) left to right, Frank Hall, Fred Pfrangley, Smith, Reg Welch, Tom Coey, Vincent Pfrangley and Ted Guy.

THE WAR MEMORIAL at the Fiveways junction, circa 1925.

Interior of ST. MICHAEL'S CHURCH, about 1930.

COLEHILL CRICKET CLUB, 1931. Seated, left to right. Ralph Habgood, Archie Guy, Mrs. Raymond, Montague Raymond (president), Austin Fripp, Doug Allen. Standing, left to right Frank Morgan, Fred Richmond, Frank Habgood, Alfred Talbot, Alf Horne, Charlie Sawtell, Jock House, Bill Sawtell and Dennis Hayward.

BEAUCROFT HOUSE, home of Sir Charles Rugge-Price, circa 1935.

COLEHILL CRICKET CLUB, about 1932. Seated, left to right Frank Middleton, Archie Guy, Frank Barrett, Austin Fripp, Ray Morgan. Standing, left to right Ron Richmond, Sid Dacombe, Charlie Brown, Reg Welch, Doug Allen, Bill Sawtell and Frank Morgan.

EAST ENDERS IN DORSET at the War Memorial, about 1934. Mrs. Digby, in her wheel-chair, is surrounded by deprived children from the East End of London, holidaying in Dorset.

COLEHILL ST. MICHAEL'S FOOTBALL CLUB, 1933 (photographed at Cuthbury, Wimborne). Seated, left to right, Fred Richmond, Harold Hansford, Ray Cleall, Charlie Stout, Charlie Sawtell. On ground, left to right, Harry Cleall, Sharky Ware. Standing, left to right, Lou Wigmore (trainer), Sam Collier, Wally Platt, Alan Hickman, Harold Hutchins, Percy Honeybun, Walter Cole and Jay.

COLEHILL CRICKET CLUB, about 1937. Seated, left to right Ralph Habgood, Reg Welch, Archie Guy, F.D.K. Rowe, Doug Allen. Standing, left to right Ern Osman, Ted Norman, Vincent, Taylor, Harold Fiander, Reg Scott, Ray Morgan, Bob Ives, Lawes and John Welch.

OPPOSITE, top
THE STRINGER FAMILY'S FLEET OF CARS, parked in the drive of North Leigh House, about 1938. Car buff Barry Cousens of Wincanton has identified the vehicles for us. On the left, JT2182 is a 6-cylinder Talbot London, designed by George Roesch, with a stone-grill in front of the radiator. GC3545 is an MG. JT4666 is a Vauxhall 14. Finally, on the right, LJ4305 is a Bournemouth-registered 12 to 14 horsepower Wolseley.

THE OLD SMITHY IN COLEHILL LANE. Generations of the Guy family ran the business, until its closure soon after the outbreak of the 1939 war. Photographed by the author in 1990.

COFFEE TAVERN IN COLEHILL LANE, which served as the village meeting place for many years. It stood originally in Lonnen Road and was dismantled and moved to its present site, where it was photographed in 1980.

SELWYN STRINGER AND HIS WIFE, outside North Leigh House, in about 1936.

MIDDLEHILL SCHOOL, circa 1938.

Chapter 8

THE THIRTIES AND THE SECOND WAR

Colehill still retained much of its rural aspect during the 'thirties. New houses were being erected, but this sort of development was on a small scale. Sims, the owner of the land on the western side of Beaucroft Lane, for example, sold it off in building plots in 1932, and provided a gravel service road for the convenience of residents, parallel with, and above, the deep narrow ravine through which motor traffic negotiates the hill along the old sunken lane.

The village is remembered as quite a busy place sixty years ago. In Wimborne Road, there were two grocery and general stores, within a few yards of each other; one was run by Miss Burling, who had inherited the business from her father. The next owner was named Brown and he, in turn, was succeeded by Reginald Joy; later, after the second war, this shop came into the ownership of Reg West and his wife; Cobb was the owner of the other and he sold the business at the end of the Great War to Frank Baldwin. At that time, it was primarily a baker's shop, with its own coke-fired ovens on the premises. Ted Baldwin followed his father into the business, baking and then delivering the bread by horse and cart over a widespread round in the district. Baldwin became the only village baker when Barrett gave up this side of his business in 1926, and later, in 1936, sold the shop to his sister, Mrs Winnie Hall, and moved the bakery business to Leigh Common to the premises previously occupied by Farrant, who had also been a baker there, more than twenty years previously. In the meantime, it had been a butcher's shop, run by James Hardiman.

Baldwin had his striking advertisement painted on the wall of his premises in 1941. It can still be seen to this day, although the bakehouse closed down more than forty years ago. Recalling his business life with remarkable clarity in his eighty-ninth year, Baldwin remembered the original painting portraying the baker very properly dressed in a *white* apron and cap. The colours must have faded over the years, with the result that the recent restoration shows these garments to be yellow.

One or two of his anecdotes of village life in the 'thirties are amusing. On one occasion, on a delivery round beyond Broomhill on the road to Holt Forest, his pony tripped in a ford swollen by heavy rain, causing the two-wheel trap to pitch forward, depositing most of its load of bread and cakes into the water. There was the customer, of a very forgetful nature, who was in the habit of summoning her dog, which had the singular name of "Kettle", by a variety of alternative names – "Saucepan", "Frying-pan" and so on. One of his jobs as a roundsman was to wring the neck of a chicken for a woman customer who was unequal to the task. He learned one of the local names for potatoes – "Tiddies" – from a customer. A roundsman employed by him, Matt Ricketts, a cheerful man with rosy red cheeks, seems to have been quite a "character", always, apparently, singing on his rounds and very much enjoying an argument, happily assuming the mantle of "Devil's Advocate" when necessary. He was still to be seen locally, delivering bread, long after Baldwin had retired, and working for a Wimborne baker until well into the 'sixties.

The two general stores in Wimborne Road remained in business into the 1970s, under a succession of new owners. Further along the road, there was a cycle shop, run by Charlie Matcham, who had moved his business from the shed behind the Coffee Tavern, and Farrant's carrier's business. The Police House was adjacent (and many years later, there was one in Middlehill Road); George Burt's tailor's shop was not far away; and Thomas Major, a builder, had extensive premises at the corner of Greenhill Road and Greenhill Close.

Bert Wareham, the cobbler, had a workshop in Merrifield, occupying the same premises as had his uncle, Jimmy, the former wheelwright. Wareham continued in business for many years.. When he retired, just over thirty years ago, the corrugated iron building of the cobbler's workshop was transported to the back garden of his sister-in-law in Lonnen Road, where it still stands, serving now as a garden shed. Barrett, the postmaster, who had earlier also run the village bakery, died in 1942 and was succeeded by his daughter, Amy, who had married Claude, one of the Roberts brothers, who farmed in Colehill Lane. Colehill Farm, leased from the Kingston Lacy Estate, extended on both sides of Colehill Lane, and on the east, abutted on to Lonnen Road. Harold and Claude Roberts took over the farm on the death of their father, Tom, in 1939. Tom Roberts had run the farm since 1922, following the death of the previous tenant, Joseph Hardy Guy.

Pilford had its own small general stores, run by Mrs Edith White, housed in a wooden hut, and the business has survived into the 'nineties, but now as a modern brick-built shop, owned by Audrey Jupe, niece of Wareham, the old shoemender. Next to Middlehill School, a very well-sited small sweet shop, owned by Frederick Saunders, who had an adjacent smallholding, had a flourishing trade. There were travelling salesmen, too, one of whom, Chewter, is remembered as one of the "characters" of the time, carrying his basket from door to door, and selling his wares, darning needles and other haberdashery. The redundant clay-pits in Smugglers Lane, which had been worked for the old Coombes brickworks, were in use as the Council's rubbish tip.

Middlehill School was still heated by coal fires in 1930. Four years later, with 163 on the roll, the girls over eleven years of age were transferred to Wimborne, so that the establishment became solely a Junior School. 1934 also saw the arrival, at last, of a water supply at the school, piped from the public mains.

The Dorset County Council took control at the end of June 1935, but the connection with the Greatheds of Uddens persisted, Major and Mrs Eric Hanbury-Tracy, of Olivers House, being two of the Trustees. Mrs Hanbury-Tracy was the granddaughter of Mary Greathed, and her son, Claude Hanbury-Tracy-Domville, in due course, inherited the Uddens Estate, on the death, in 1952, of his aunt, Mrs Elizabeth Oldfield, eldest daughter of Sir Edward

Harris Greathed. The school continued to benefit, and still does, from Mary Greathed's Endowment. An attempt, in 1936, by the County Council, to use some of the proceeds from the Endowment for the benefit of other schools was thwarted.

The Parish Council continued to meet at the Coffee Tavern, still owned by Joseph Edward Guy, in the 'thirties. Barrett became the Chairman, and Hay was among the other councillors; so too was the Vicar, Stote, until his resignation in 1934, when Major Eric Hanbury-Tracy took his place. The Major is remembered as a man with a rather high-pitched voice, and was small of stature, unlike his son, Claude, who was to carry on the family tradition of public service locally with much distinction after the war.

Two issues seem to have occupied much of their time, the question of boundary changes, and a matter related to it, the deplorable state of Leigh Common. There was a suggestion that Colehill should merge with Hampreston and West Parley to create a new Urban District. This idea, fifty or sixty years ahead of its time, fell through. And the Council successfully resisted the attempts of the Wimborne Urban District Council to encroach upon Colehill's territory. A letter in the Western Gazette from the secretary of the Wimborne Ratepayers' Association read: "Colehill is clamouring for improvements in their drainage system as well as benefits to be derived from urbanisation." Frank Barrett commented, at a Council meeting: "The case is quite the reverse and any attempt on this parish by the Wimborne Urban Council will undoubtedly be met by strong opposition from the parish."

The tipping of rubbish on Leigh Common was causing concern, as it had done before, and has done since. But the main problem on the common was Leigh Pond, which was being fouled by drainage and sewage from Wimborne and had become offensively smelly.

For the rest, the Parish Council continued to debate and reject street lighting, whether by gas or electricity – overhead cables supplied electric current to properties in Wimborne Road in 1933, and electricity reached domestic consumers at the top of what was then Leigh Lane three years later. Refuse collection, with a reference to a 21 years lease on the existing Parish rubbish dump on the site of the old Coombes brickyard, and main drainage were also discussed, as far back as 1934. Incidentally, R.J.N. Willcox, the engineer historian, who has been quoted on old roads earlier in this account, was called in to give an expert opinion on the drainage scheme. He had made his home in the old Beaucroft Dairy Cottage in the early 'thirties, and lived there until his death many years after the war.

Curiously, a later occupant of the cottage, Colonel George Gray, is another student of local history and he has given considerable help in researching material for this narrative, especially in the loan of old deeds and other documents.

The parish councillors, having discussed all these modern amenities at some length, decided against them all. On the face of it, and with hindsight, these men stand indicted as a group of backward-looking reactionaries. However, it must be remembered that these amenities, which we regard as necessities, no doubt appeared to them, serving a rural community, as expensive luxuries; they were, after all, trustees of public funds, just as District Councillors, County Councillors, and indeed, the Government are. Nor did matters lie solely within their own competence. The Rural District Council, on which Colehill was represented by Hanbury-Tracy and Miss Martha Main, familiarly known as "Matty" and prominent in the Girl Guide movement in Wimborne, was hardly more progressive, and neighbouring Parish Councils were very much involved with the decisions on drainage and refuse collection. On the matter of street lighting, the council were dealing with private companies, the Wimborne Gas Company and the Bournemouth and Poole Electricity Company, who were in business for profit, and who were not prepared to make a loss in providing lamp standards and the necessary maintenance. On balance, in any case, the views of the village people seem to have been fairly expressed by their elected representatives.

The Bournemouth Gas and Water Company had taken over the supply of those commodities from the original authorities by the mid-'thirties. As the decade drew to its close, the Council continued to debate the same contentious issues, until the approach of war enabled them to shelve matters "for the duration". Wimborne's determined bid to annex Colehill had been successfully resisted. The question of a burial ground for the village, a matter which had apparently been permanently laid to rest at the beginning of the century, cropped up again briefly in 1938 and was then forgotten. One issue of much interest to the village was raised in the previous year, when steps were put in hand to create a public recreation ground.

The obvious site was the village football ground, owned by Bert Cole. Cole was willing to sell his field, and the Bankes Estate was willing to sell an adjoining strip of land, but inexplicably, the Council, in spite of a probable grant from the King George V Playing Fields Fund, decided not to proceed. It is interesting to note that the matter of tree preservation was on the Council's agenda as long ago as 1938 and that road hazards, which we tend to think of as a modern problem, were causing concern in that same year, when the crossroads at the Church was described as dangerous.

The Council also had to administer the proceeds of Gundry's Charity, one-fifth of which, amounting to eight shillings per annum, came to the Overseers of the Poor of the Parish of Colehill. Eight needy individuals received a shilling each.

The rest of the Council's time seems to have been occupied with dealing with complaints of a trifling nature from some of the local gentry. Mrs Farrer, of Park Homer, for example, seems to have taken a somewhat high-handed attitude towards the Council with regard to the overgrown public footpath adjoining her property, and to have claimed a right to direct authorities as to what should, and what should not, be cleared. She also complained of "wheeled" traffic (in the form of bicycles and prams) making use of the path, to which access was gained, at that time, through a kissing-gate at the upper end.

Kelly's Directory for 1935 recorded that Frank Barrett was still the Postmaster – telephone number: Wimborne 22 – as well as running his grocery business. There was still a dairyman in Little Lonnen, Joe Guy was still the blacksmith and David Cobb was still selling boots. There were smallholders at Middle Hill, a farmer at Pilford Heath and a market gardener at Four Wells Nursery. Major Frank Hyde ran "The Jockey House" – one of the "Road Houses" fashionable at that time – at Leigh Common, and John Loveridge was licensee of the "Barley Mow", at the other side of the hill.

The 1939 Directory showed scarcely any changes. As for the occupants of the big houses in that last year of peace, Charles Hay still lived at Rowney, the Sollys at Bells, the Truells at Onslow, the Hanbury-Tracys at Olivers and Mrs Lonsdale, born Katherine Glyn, at The Further House. Selwyn Stringer was at North Leigh and Mrs Farrer lived at Park Homer. Beaucroft was the residence of Sir Charles Rugge-Price, the seventh Baronet, his wife, Lady Isabella, and his family, two sons and two daughters, Marjorie and Lois. Rugge-Price had emigrated from across the Irish Sea, and brought his staff of Irish servants with him. His chauffeur was George Jackson, who lived in the flat over the garage converted from the old stables and coach-house. George's nephew, Merrick Jackson, later became the Clerk to the Parish Council, a post he held for many years, and he also served the Rural District Council as Deputy Clerk.

The Cricket Club continued to flourish throughout the 'thirties, managed by a dedicated committee, on which Ralph Habgood, secretary for several years, Archie Guy, Reg Welch and Frank Barrett were especially prominent. Guy was employed at the Waterworks at Walford; Habgood also worked there before moving to the electricity Power Station in Poole; and Welch was an engineer at the Eclipse Works in Wimborne before becoming caretaker at the Middlehill School. Habgood, Guy and Welch were also among the leading players of that decade before the second war, which culminated in the Club winning the Championship of the Bournemouth and District League in 1938. Other stalwarts on the field of play were Charlie Sawtell, Frank Middleton and Doug Allen. The latter was prominent in village affairs at a later date, serving on the Parish Council after the war. He was a founder member of the local RAF Association.

A dressing room was erected at the ground in 1933, with the blessing of the owner, Mrs Solly, and her tenant, Coakes. The labour for this was provided by members who were unemployed, a sign of the times. Sir Charles Rugge-Price joined the list of Vice-Presidents in the late 'thirties.

Even as early as July 1937, the threat of a new war had made an impact on the village, classes for first-aid instruction for Air Raid Precautions volunteers being started. A year later, the Log Book of the Girl Guides records that they had to change their normal meeting place "as the hall was occupied by soldiers" – presumably members of the Territorial Army; again, in the following February: "Poppy Patrol went to be patients for the A.R.P. workers." Selwyn Stringer was appointed Chief Air Warden for Colehill, in October 1938. One of the last meetings of the Parish Council at their old home, the Coffee Tavern, was in July 1939, the premises being requisitioned by the Army on the outbreak of war, and meetings during the war being held at a variety of venues, but usually at Rowney House, the home of Charles Hay. The Coffee Tavern was released by the military in 1942, and the Parish Council returned there briefly, holding one meeting there in April 1944.

Troops were stationed at Colehill in 1940, in the early months of the war, being billeted compulsorily at any properties with vacant rooms, Rowney House and Park Homer, both of which have been demolished since the war, among them; and some were accommodated under canvas on the Middlehill School playing field. North Leigh House and its grounds were used for similar purposes, and the remains of a wartime supply of coal for heating the house was discovered many years afterwards. The King's Dragoon Guards and the Middlesex Regiment made their home in the upper part of the village and the Royal Hussars were well represented in the area around Leigh Lane and Leigh Common.

"The Jockey House" hostelry at Leigh Common saw use as a canteen for the troops, and the Church Hall seems to have been turned into a recreation room and canteen for the benefit of the soldiers, and was well patronised by them. Among those cooking and serving "innumerable snacks of eggs and beans" were "Jimmy" Hewett and Margot Sinclair. By September 1940, the Hall was serving as an ARP Station. The Parish Magazine for that month recorded that, during the Church Garden Party, "the Chief Warden gave warning of machine-gunning in the near neighbourhood". Other sources speak of a German fighter machine-gunning properties in Hayes Lane. All fingerposts identifying the location were removed during the "invasion scare" and the name of the village was obliterated from boundary stones and from the War Memorial. The potential danger of roadside gorse being ignited by enemy action and being a fire hazard, especially around Wimborne Road, Cobbs Road and Jenny Down, was foreseen by the authorities, and steps taken to cut it back.

Meanwhile, the Church Authorities were considering the installation of electric lighting, but decided to defer the matter until after the war. At the Horns Inn, Commander Heathcote succeeded Captain Worley, who had returned to the Army, as the landlord.

The Cricket Club remained active during the early years of the war, playing "friendly" matches. The Annual Meetings now took place at Rowney House, the home of the President, Charlie Hay. At a meeting in April 1941, "the future policy of the Club in the light of the National Emergency was discussed at some length. As there was so much Military in the neighbourhood and surrounding districts, it was agreed that the object of the Club should be to provide as much entertainment as possible for the troops, and with this in mind, it was unanimously decided to carry on."

Henry Habgood and Joe Guy were still active, and were the club's umpires. Food rationing precluded the provision of teas at cricket matches for the future. The tenancy of the cricket field had passed from Coakes to George Humphries. The 1942 meeting resolved to carry on in spite of "increasing difficulties under existing war conditions, if only to provide entertainment for local troops".

Already there was a record of one member killed on active service and one missing. The club was unable to continue after 1942 until the end of the war, and it seems that the local ARP used the cricket pavilion, sited, in those days, on the northern side of the ground, as their headquarters.

Farrant's old garage, in Wimborne Road, was pressed into service as a makeshift fire station, but there appears to have been little damage inflicted on the village during air raids. No doubt, the navigators in the German bombers found the railway line useful for identifying their position on moonlit nights, and the vast area of glass at the adjoining Leigh Vineries must have been a prominent landmark. A few bombs fell, near Hayes Lane, and in Leigh Lane, near the railway, where a thatched cottage was destroyed; they were dropped, presumably, from German bombers which had failed to find their target during attacks on places such as Yeovil, Bristol and Cardiff, and were returning through the skies of Dorset to their bases in France. According to one version of the incident, an aerial landmine parachuted down uncomfortably close to the Horns Inn, which had been rebuilt only some twenty years earlier, after the original thatched inn had been destroyed by fire.

Frank Peckham remembered both incidents. There was the fire of 1923, when Charles Bull, the licensee, carried on his business from an old army hut, while the premises were rebuilt – before he committed suicide – and also the wartime explosion. His own cottage, near the Horns, was damaged, and rendered temporarily uninhabitable, in this, caused, not by a landmine, but by one of two bombs which exploded in the road outside his garden gate, creating a vast crater. Cannon Hill, in those years before the view was obstructed by the trees, became a splendid "grandstand" for the intrepid youths of the village to watch the explosions and fires as Southampton was bombed.

Both Leigh Vineries and Jenny Down became parks for tanks at one stage during the conflict, and before the Allied invasion of Normandy, United States troops were camped on Jenny Down under canvas, as well as being billetted at Park Homer and Beaucroft, the latter thus fulfilling a military function for the second time in its history. The grounds of Beaucroft were used as a park for American artillery and their tanks were parked in Highland Road. A "PX" was housed in a building at the corner of Beaucroft Road and Wimborne Road, for supplying cigarettes and other essentials for civilised living to the U.S. soldiers. Earlier in the war, there had been complaints of damage to the roads by British military vehicles; and now the Americans were being blamed for similar damage, to Cobbs Road and Wimborne Road; and around Leigh Common, where the Jockey House, later destroyed by fire, was still requisitioned by the military.

The Americans went away and Colehill, far removed from the firing line of "Flying Bombs" and V2 Rockets, returned to its former self, awaiting the return of its menfolk. Not all came back, when the war came to an end in 1945: more names had to be added to those inscribed on the village War Memorial. Those who returned were to see vast changes in the years that followed.

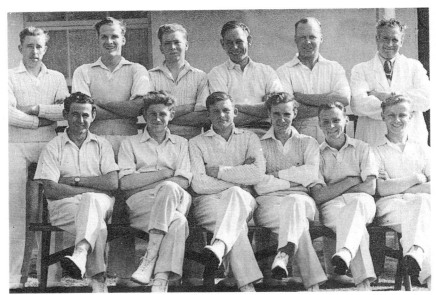

COLEHILL CRICKET CLUB, 1948. Seated, left to right Gerry Hoare, Ken Mullett, Jim Welch, Tony Ashley, Stan Richmond, Brian Morgan. Standing, left to right Fred Norman, Frank Bray, John Slow, George Budden, Pat O'Hara and Charlie Sawtell (umpire).

COLEHILL MOTHERS' UNION BRANCH Jubilee Gathering at the old Vicarage 1949. Front row. Miss Benison, Mrs. Page Phillips, Miss Salt, Mrs. Gardner, Mrs. Jackson, Kilmister, Mrs. Fray, Mrs. Shipton, Mrs. Boyt, Mrs. Sweatland, Mrs. Monk. Second row, Mrs. Humphries, Mrs. Chappell, Mrs. Willcox, Miss Whinchcombe, Mrs. Raymond, Rev. J.E. Price, Mrs. Key, Canon Stote-Blandy, Mrs. Lunt, Bishop Key, Mrs. Stote-Blandy, Mrs. Price, Mrs. Cox, Mrs. Hatchard, Mrs. B. Hayward, Mrs. F. Hall, Mrs. Taylor, Mrs. Burgess. Third row, Mrs. D. Bryant, Mrs. Roberts, Miss Martin, Mrs. Christopher, Mrs. Cole, Mrs. Whitcombe, Mrs. Clarke, Mrs. W. Richmond, Mrs. Price, Mrs. Woodhams, Mrs. Lambourne, Mrs. Benham, Mrs. Kerley, Mrs. W. Hayward, Mrs. Morfett, Mrs. A. Frampton, Mrs. Hansford, Mrs. Baldwin, Mrs. V. Hall, Mrs. Redfern. Back row. Miss Knott, Mrs. Batten, Mrs. J. Hunt, Mrs. F. Richmond, Miss Dare, Miss James, Mrs. Furnell, Mrs. Fripp, Miss James, Mrs. Cooper, Mrs. Carden, Mrs. Vi Moore, Mrs. White and Mrs. H. Richmond.

OPPOSITE
GIRL GUIDES, about 1955. Seated, left to right Mabel Digby, Margaret Pope, Irene Smart, Jimmy Hewett, Barbara Roberts, Margaret Hulbert, Mrs. Price. Kneeling, left to right, Jennifer Peckham, ?, Jane Hammond, Rachel Pope, Susan Angel. Standing on chairs (back row) left to right Kathleen White, ?, Diane Scott, ?, ?, Janice Legg, ?, June Hammond. Standing (second row) left to right, Brenda Boast, Ann Boast, Gillian Moore, Margaret Ferguson, Margaret Brake, Violet Angel and Margaret Till.

GIRL GUIDES about 1960. Left to right M. Donovan, Sue Scott, Jimmy Hewett, Ann Legg and Stella Boyt.

OPPOSITE, top
THE FIRST HOME OF THE METHODISTS ON COLEHILL, Chapel Cottage, from the air circa 1975. Above the cottage, adjoining the track, can be seen the remains of the clay-pit used for the original brick kiln.

OPPOSITE, bottom
CHAPEL COTTAGE, from the ground in 1990.

BELLS HOUSE in 1990.

OPPOSITE
FRANK BALDWIN'S ADVERTISEMENT outside his old bakery at Leigh Common, photographed by Rodney Legg in 1991. This was originally painted in 1941.

Chapter 9

MODERN TIMES

We have seen how Colehill grew, in the space of about one hundred years, from a scattered population, living in humble cottages – those "wild and lawless" people encountered by Colonel Paget up on the heath – to a self-contained village, with its own School, Church and Parish Council. It was obviously regarded as what would have been termed a very "select" place in which to live, for it attracted a considerable number of people from the top echelons of society. High ranking officers in the Army, some Generals among them, and the Royal Navy; and clergymen, as well as other professional men, came to the village when they retired: Knights of the Realm, some of them with local affiliations, and others with aristocratic connections made it their home.

They purchased their large plots of land for their houses, set in their own extensive grounds, from the landed gentry, the Bankes, Hanham and Greathed families who, between them, had owned this part of Dorset for centuries past. They engaged servants to staff their establishments from the local population, and tradesmen and craftsmen set up in business to cater for the needs of the emerging village.

In its way, it was almost a feudal society, certainly before the Great War. The combined effect of estate duties and a general change in the expectations of the common people gradually resulted in rather less sharply defined class distinctions after 1918, and yet on Colehill, the old ways persisted largely unaltered. At least one of the "grand ladies" in the village still expected, and received, curtsies from the women she passed in the street, and the touching of forelocks from the men.

A variety of occupations were followed in the village. Wimborne was near enough to provide employment for many, especially after the opening of Sir Alan Cobham's Flight Refuelling factory early in the 'thirties, and a lot of men were engaged in agriculture, at the various farms, smallholdings and nurseries in and around Colehill. One resident was a chef on the celebrated "Pines Express"; Miss Osman's father was an engine-driver on the Somerset and Dorset Railway. The staffing of the "Big Houses" by no means monopolised all the available labour in the village.

However, even in the years following 1945, the same pattern of society persisted, perhaps in a rather more diluted form. The aristocracy was still represented in Colehill. Rowney House, formerly the home of Charles Hay, became the residence of Rev the Honourable Andrew Charles Victor Elphinstone, who was Curate at Wimborne Minster shortly after the war. He was descended from the Bowes-Lyon family on his mother's side, being the second son of the sixteenth Baron Elphinstone, who had married a daughter of the Earl of Strathmore, and was a cousin of the Queen, to whom his wife became Lady-in-Waiting; Colehill was thus given its only connection with the Royal Family.

Not far from the home of the original Pagets, at Park Homer, a couple of generations before, Reverend Sir and Lady Paget Bowman came to live at The Further House, renamed "Joldwynds", formerly the home of Mrs Lonsdale, a member of the Glyn family, and related, through marriage, to the Greatheds. The Wimborne and District News, reporting the death, early in 1952, of Mrs Elizabeth Oldfield (née Greathed) commented: "... it typifies the passing of an age – the age of leisure and the last days of feudalism... The spacious days are fast fading into memories."

Times were indeed changing, and Colehill, at last, was changing with them. The subtleties of class distinction eventually vanished with the tremendous influx of newcomers which flooded into the village from 1960 onwards. Many of these were young couples, just raising their families, but a considerable number were retired folk. Colehill still attracted a number of retired military and naval officers, who took an active part in village, and especially Church, affairs.

As recently as 1970, the casual observer might have supposed, reading the names of the members of the Parochial Church Council, that their meetings were really conferences of the Chiefs of Staff planning a Combined Operation! The Royal Air Force was represented by one senior officer, while the Army had two representatives; the Senior Service also had two, including the Vicar, Charles Raynor-Smith.

But village affairs had largely revolved around the axis of the Anglican and Methodist Churches, and social and sporting activities had largely sprung from them. The School, the Scouts and the Guides were all interwoven into this self-contained society, and Colehill, not a tight community in the geographical sense, was, nevertheless, very much an integrated village. All of this gradually changed over the years as "the invaders" swamped the native (or at least, long established) residents with their vast numbers, so that the population of Colehill grew to a size considerably larger than that of Wimborne itself. At the same time, the number of people actually *working* in the village has declined to a mere handful.

The result is, in essence, a vast dormitory suburb of Wimborne – indeed, perhaps more accurately, of Bournemouth and Poole. Near universal ownership of television sets and motor cars, those two anti-social manifestations of the late twentieth century, has caused people either to find their recreation at home, or to seek it beyond the confines of their own parish. The Evening Women's Institute (founded in the late 'sixties – the original one, which met in the afternoons, is now defunct, another sign of changing times) alone proclaims the identity of Colehill in a social sense; it, and the Cricket Club, which has widened its activities to spawn the "Colehill Sports and Social Club". The children attend one of several schools in the village – there are no fewer than six of these now, with the comparatively recent arrival of Dumpton – if, indeed, they do not have to go beyond the boundaries of the parish for their education. Perhaps, after all, it is the Church which remains the focal point of what survives of the population's local allegiance.

Things were very different in those early years after the war. Water and gas were available (although not for all – piped water from the mains lay nearly twenty years ahead for some); there was no street lighting; and there was no mains sewerage, nor would there be for another fifteen years. Several roads still had a gravel surface, and there were few pavements for the convenience of pedestrians. From the vantage point of today, it all seems rather primitive.

The Rural District Council started a household refuse collection in the village – once every *five* weeks – in 1946; the frequency became three weeks in the following year. The naming of more roads was given "official" blessing by the Parish Council in 1949: many roads had been "officially" named, as we have noted, twenty years previously and had been given name plates, but others bore alternative names and it became convenient, especially to the postal authorities, to decide upon something specific.

Old habits die hard, however, and there are references subsequently, even in the Council Minutes as late as 1960, to "Donkey Lane", the name for the path running up to St Audrey's, from Burts Hill, and to the adjacent "Curtis Hill". Similarly, other roads and locations were still identified by the names of people farming or living in the neighbourhood. Thus, the junction at the bottom of "Church Hill", once known as "Bown's Corner", became "Cole's Corner"; "Roberts' Hill" was another name for Little Lonnen. In 1952, the upper part of Canford Bottom, above the Hayes Lane junction, was renamed Middlehill Road and the trunk road, running past Leigh Common, called Ringwood Road previously, became Leigh Road.

The first visible signs of change in the village after the war were, on the one hand, the erection, in 1950, of the council houses near the Church, in Colehill Lane – Marshfield, on the eastern side; and at a later date, New Merrifield opposite – and the demolition of two of the larger houses, Park Homer, which was converted into flats before its demise, and Rowney. Both were replaced by little estates of modest houses, the former remembering in the names of roads both the house and its original owner. There was a link between the old and the new, many of the occupants of the flats at Park Homer, pulled down in the late 'fifties, being rehoused at Marshfield. One of them, Dick Selby, in the building trade, had the distinction of being employed in the demolition of his old home, before helping to build the new houses on the site. His father, Walter Selby, was for many years the road sweeper in Colehill, his especial pride being his Saturday task of keeping the road between the War Memorial and the Church in immaculate condition for the churchgoers the following day.

Quarry Corner has also vanished, again, several smaller properties replacing the one house in its own grounds. Olivers House, renamed Stroud Lodge, when purchased by Miss Marsh, who converted it into a "Retirement Home", survived a little longer, and is commemorated by the names of new roads which serve the large housing estate which runs down the hill from the first village school to the track-bed of the old railway line in the valley below.

The big houses which have survived, Bells, Highlands and Onslow, have been converted into spacious flats; Beaucroft was divided into three self-contained houses in 1953, after ownership of it and its 31-acre estate had passed from Sir Charles Rugge-Price, first to Miss Marjorie Alderton, and then to a limited company, Beaucroft Estate Ltd.; only North Leigh and one or two others remain as complete private houses. One of them, Crabb House, was the home of the celebrated golfer, Peter Alliss, for a brief period, after the death of Sir Richard Glyn. There was talk, in 1947, of another, The Further House, becoming a Night Club, which caused some consternation in the neighbourhood; however, it was no more than a rumour. Onslow House still has a memento of its former glory, in the days of its first owners, the Truells. A boundary stone, marking the limits of its extensive grounds, remains in Giddylake, down the hill from the house, inscribed "R.H.T. 1884".

The first years of peace witnessed changes, physical and otherwise, in the Church. Stote-Blandy, the historian parson, a Canon of Salisbury Cathedral, resigned the living after a tenure of twenty-eight years. He was succeeded as Vicar by an ex-Army Chaplain, John Price, in 1946. Among the laymen (and women) active in Church affairs in the postwar years were Sir Richard Glyn, Rupert Keable, Rowley Raymond and Sister D.R. Dare, the District Nurse.

The long-awaited electric lighting, the subject of occasional debate for the best part of thirty years, was eventually installed in the Church and Hall in 1950.

After a reign of twelve years, Price retired as Vicar in 1958, and died only a few months afterwards. His successor was Rev W.L. Dobb, who remained in office for only three years, being followed by Charles Raynor-Smith in March 1962. Among other names closely associated with St Michael's around this time were Stanley Weedon, Charles Osborne, a retired Commander in the Royal Navy, and George Gray, a retired R.E.M.E. Lieutenant-Colonel. Charles Sawtell, after nearly 40 years' service ringing the Church bells, resigned as Captain of the Ringers in 1968.

The Methodist Church changed over to electric lighting in 1961. New faces had arrived to help sustain the fortunes of the chapel, notable among them being Reg Scott, soon after the war, Pat and Marjorie Cailes, and at a later date, John and Molly Slow. The appointment of a Deaconess, Pamela Le Poidevin – "Sister Pam" – in 1962, gave the church a resident minister, for the first time. She stayed in the village for eight years, living next to the church in a caravan. The site of her home is now occupied by the Church Hall, now used as a meeting place by several organisations.

New advertisers in the Parish Magazine by the end of the 'fifties had included Burt and Randall, tailors in Green Hill Road, David Cobb, practising as a chiropodist and masseur and running a gentlemen's hairdressing business from the little shop beside his home in Wimborne Road, the Heatherview Filling Station, owned by M.W. and G.W. Drinkwater – Colehill Service Station, on the same site, is still with us – and Colehill Shoe Repair Service, at the "Corner Shop", now demolished, at the junction of Beaucroft Road and Wimborne Road. This building had previously been the electrical repair workshop of Nisbet, and earlier, during the war, had served as the American "PX", supplying the U.S. soldiers with cigarettes and chewing gum.

Ron Jones purchased the garage business in Wimborne Road from the Drinkwaters, running it for several years until his retirement, and he became prominent in village affairs. The garage in Wimborne Road is the only surviving business in what had once been, in a modest way, a fairly busy trading thoroughfare. The two general stores remained in business until the 'seventies. Reg West and his wife owned one of them for several years following the war. They made a point of flying the Union Jack above their shop on such occasions as Empire Day and the Coronation of the Queen. David Cobb carried on his hairdressing business almost as long.

At the rear of his house in the Holmsley Villas terrace, Reg Shiner ran a cobbler's business. A small general stores was opened by Lindsay and Leslie Kerr in a conversion of the old Manager's house on the old Leigh Vineries when the new housing estate was built there, but this closed down after a few years. The only other new shops in the village – and these have all survived – are those in the small parade in Middlehill Road, built in the grounds of Park Homer, when the house was demolished. Of the old village shops, dating back to the turn of the century, only two remain – the Post Office Stores, in the centre of the village, and the Handy Stores, in Pilford. The Post Office, run by two generations of Barretts, Frank and his daughter, Amy (who had become Mrs Roberts), had scarcely changed in the seventy years since it opened in 1897, and many will remember it as a small, ill-lit shop, before it was taken over by John and Mary Dacombe, who enlarged and modernised the premises.

There was a proposal by the Blandford brewers, Hall and Woodhouse, to purchase "Beechwood", at the War Memorial "Fiveways", in the early 'sixties, with a view to converting it into a public house. Persistent efforts by the brewers to obtain a licence met with determined opposition from the Parish Council and the plan was eventually dropped. Such a conversion would, in any case, have been a breach of a Covenant, expressly forbidding the use of any building on the plot of land as an inn or hotel, although neither the brewers nor their opponents seem to have been aware of this.

Part of the rural aspect of the village survived the pillaging of the "developers" in the post-war years, and indeed, still does so, especially on the northern slopes of the hill, in the Greenhill and Pilford districts.

The Bankes Estate leased Colehill Farm, in Colehill Lane, to the Roberts brothers, Claude and Harold. Harold used to deliver milk from the farm by motorbike and sidecar. Claude's daughter, Margaret, married Derek Pope, and they eventually took over the lease. When Oakley Burgess retired from Long Lane Farm, another Bankes property, the leases were amalgamated, and the Popes ran the two farms as one.

Both farms have now gone, but the fields, inherited by the National Trust, remain. Frank Peckham remained in business at Brickyard Farm, albeit in a small way, until his death in 1991: he used to graze his cattle in a field adjoining Highland Road, and on the Beaucroft Estate not many years ago, and at another time, in the fields between Leigh Lane and Northleigh Lane; and there was a piggery in the field next to Beaucroft House.

No English village is complete without its cast of "characters", and Colehill is no exception. Some of the older ones have already been mentioned, but there were others who appeared on the scene in the post-war years. One of these, a bespectacled man in a trilby hat, with Oriental connections, was, first a regular visitor to his sister in Lonnen Road, and eventually came to live with her on a permanent basis. He was frequently to be seen around the village, in a somewhat unkempt condition as a result of the parrot on his shoulder, which kept him permanent company. There was the bearded individual known to all as "Maurice", an enthusiastic walker, who was reputed to live at Gaunts, and who made a daily pilgrimage for his tipple at The Barley

Mow, where he had his favourite chair, which always had to be vacated on his arrival.

The diminutive Frederick Angel, who lived in Beaucroft Lane, was gardener at The Croft, the house opposite the cricket ground, for 40 years, thereby earning a long-service medal from the Royal Horticultural Society. This was the home of the Raymond family, when he started work there, and he was still tending the garden during the years when George Gray and his family were resident. Gray was active in the Scout movement locally and threw open his garden to the Cub pack and the boys' parents on one occasion. Angel was still at his work, and could be seen, bespectacled, and as always, wearing his cap, threading his way across the lawn among these young lads, no taller than any of them. No doubt "characters" in their own right, but especially remembered as a "star turn" much in demand at local concerts, cricket dinners and the like was the amusing "double act" of Reg Welch, dressed as a Dorset countryman, and John Cutler, billed as "The Topical Two".

The Football Club appears to have been revived in 1957, having lapsed several years previously. Colehill United F.C. was the name of the re-formed club, but it was unable to find a pitch in the village, and the "home" matches were played at Leigh Park. The club was unfortunately once again disbanded within two or three years, due, apparently, to a dispute among the membership as to its name. There has since been a further revival, playing as "Colehill Sports Club", but again, their ground is outside the village, and the club plays at Holt.

This club is part of the Colehill Sports and Social Club, successor to the Colehill Cricket and Social Club. When the activities of that organisation were formally split, the Colehill Cricket Club reverted solely to its original role of catering for the summer game. In a sense, the wheel has turned full circle, the original football and cricket clubs having started side by side from their Church origins, and the modern Football Club having risen from the ashes of the old, directly as a result of the widening activities of the cricketers.

The Cricket Club resumed operations with the minumum of delay after the war, a Meeting being held at the home of the President, Hay, who had moved to Colehill Lodge, in December 1945. Two stalwarts, Joe Guy, who had been actively associated with the club for thirty years, and Frank Barrett, its first Treasurer, had died during the war, but the other familiar faces from the pre-war days were present. The club was playing again in the following summer, with most of its players having returned to civilian life, some having served with much distinction in the armed forces. Frank Middleton saw service with the Queen's Own Dorset Yeomanry and the Royal Army Service Corps, was Mentioned in Despatches, and was awarded the Belgian Croix de Guerre. There was such an abundance of talent among the cricketers that no fewer than three of them, Middleton, Rowley Raymond and Cecil Hatchard, were chosen to play for Dorset in the Minor Counties Championship. These remain Colehill's only representatives chosen for the County, with the exception, much more recently, of Richard Scott, who, in fact, was to become a professional cricketer, playing First Class cricket for Hampshire and Gloucestershire. Although having no connection with the local club, one of the teachers at the Beaucroft School, Kay Green, played at the highest level of women's cricket, representing England in a Test Match and in a World Cup series.

The Colehill Club was experiencing anxieties over its tenure of the ground soon after the war. Hopes were still being voiced in 1946 that a recreation ground might be laid out in the village; the Parish Council had shelved the matter on the outbreak of war, but was now suggesting that the site behind the old Vicarage on the Bankes Plantation, usually known as Jenny Down, might be suitable. Nothing came of this idea, although the next generation was, in fact, to see this area become the playing fields of the new St Michael's School, and indeed, has been used by the Cricket Club for some of its matches. But, in spite of much more debate in the last forty-five years, the village is still waiting for its public recreation ground.

Mrs Solly, the owner of the cricket ground, died in 1947, which raised further doubts about the Club's future there. Further trouble arose from the refusal of Humphries, the tenant farmer, to allow the mowing of the outfield. A player of that era has recalled the perils of fielding in the deep in long grass where cattle had grazed shortly before.

Colonel Rex Solly, a Vice-President of the Club, who had inherited the property, indicated that the renewal of the tenancy of the ground might be doubtful after the 1949 season, and in February of that year, stated that the property was on the market. The club did, in fact, complete its fixtures for both the 1949 and 1950 seasons with this threat of impending eviction hanging over it. The Bells House Estate was sold at the end of the 1950 summer, and the new co-owners, represented by Mr Bolton, invited offers from the club for a separate sale of the cricket ground. The happy ending to this worrying saga came in January 1951, when the ground was purchased for the club for £575, in the names of four Trustees, Albert White, a builder at Greenhill, in the same trade as Major, his predecessor in the same premises, Arthur Fripp, an estate agent, whose father, Austin, had been the club's opening batsman for many years, Reg Welch and Ralph Habgood, and mortgaged to Montague Raymond for £375.

Two curious conditions were attached to the sale. The Solly family retained ownership of the splendid oak trees fringing the field at its northern end, and indeed, these still remain their property. A request to fell them in 1958 was refused. The other unusual stipulation was that the club should remain sole owners of the ground for the following 3,000 years, a term which will take us somewhat beyond the scope of this history!

Reg Welch, Rev Sir Paget Bowman and Sir Richard and Lady Glyn were among the new Vice-Presidents in these critical years, and the committee which steered the club so successfully through this anxious time included seven who had, in 1952, collectively served the club for a total of 166 years, Archie Guy, Doug Allen, and Henry and Ralph Habgood, father and son, among them. Charlie Sawtell joined the committee, and so too did the Welch brothers, Jim and John, sons of Reg. A relative newcomer to the village, Reg Scott, also served the club as a committee-man, and was the first of three generations of Scotts to play for the club with much distinction. Andy, a son, took nine wickets for no runs in a match against Christchurch in 1958, and three of *his* sons have followed him, including Richard, a county cricketer.

Other outstanding players of the 'fifties included Frank Middleton, Ralph Habgood, John Welch, Harold Fiander, Dixie Williams and Derek Pope. An unusual fixture in the 1954 season was that between the Colehill Ladies and the Leigh Park Club Ladies. Archie Guy's reign as Club Captain, spanning 28 years, came to an end in 1955. In 1956, Charlie Hay gave up the Presidency in view of his age and poor health, but he continued his association with the club as Vice-President. In his valedictory speech, he commented that now that he "was going on the shelf", he could look back and reflect on "the great part cricket has played in the English way of life. It was the saving grace in a graceless age". Changing times, indeed!

Rowley Raymond became the new President. Around this time, a number of private schools then flourishing in the locality, Melverley, Manor House and St Cuthberga's Convent, used the ground for Sports Day and so on. Sir Richard Glyn died early in 1960: the club minutes record: "The Club, and indeed, the whole district, has lost its greatest benefactor, a very generous supporter, perhaps the most generous benefactor in the Club's history."

On a happier note, the club won the Championship of the Bournemouth and District League in the following summer, repeating this success in 1964, and no fewer than four times more in the following nine years. There was a change of scene at the northern end of the ground, the site of the old pavilion, beyond the line of trees, in 1961, when the vista of open fields disappeared and the new road, Boundary Drive, was put in, and the houses lining it were built. The son of Joseph Edward, Archie Guy, such a mainstay of the club throughout his life, as player and administrator, died in 1965. He had played cricket for Colehill since long before the Great War.

But as the old faces departed, new ones emerged to ensure the club's future, which became ever more ambitious. The club did much to encourage young cricketers, as the local population grew, and this, in a very practical way, has helped to secure its future. Ralph Habgood and Jim Welch were prominent on an energetic committee which raised funds for the building of a splendid new pavilion and clubhouse, Ron Jones became the President and Peter Alliss, when he lived in the village, was a Vice-President. By 1972, the Club had widened its horizons still further and had become the "Colehill Cricket and Social Club". The club's accounts, which had shown an income of just over £7 in 1912, recorded a corresponding figure of £6,355 sixty years later. The club has been ambitious, too, on the cricket field, and very successful, being winners of the Dorset Senior Club Championship six times in eight successive seasons during the 1980s, ensuring fame for the village in sporting circles.

The Boy Scout Troop, too, had been restarted after the war, under the leadership of Colonel J.C. Coombes, in 1948, having lapsed nineteen years earlier. The first Colehill Cub Pack was started at the same time, meeting at the Parish Hall. This revival seems to have been short-lived. However, a fresh start was made and George Bundy became Scoutmaster in 1951. Both Scouts and Cubs moved in that year to their new headquarters, the old Smithy in Colehill Lane, which had been unused and empty for ten years. The revival of the Movement locally only lasted for a few years, and it remained dormant until it was restarted in 1964, again with its headquarters at the old blacksmith's workshop, which was to remain its home for several years.

The old smith's forge remained as evidence of the building's former use, and was put to good use for fires for heating the premises in the winter months. During their sojourn there, the Scouts discovered a derelict cast-iron tyring platform, manufactured at the Poole Foundry, lying in the undergrowth behind the building. This equipment was used for fastening waggon wheels, while the metal tyre was fitted to the rim, and was probably more likely to be found at a backsmith's workshop than at the wheelwright's. The happy chance of Colonel George Gray being associated with both the Scouts and the Priest's House Museum, in Wimborne, has resulted in this artefact, bearing the inscription "S. Lewin, Maker, Poole", being preserved, to become one of the Museum's exhibits. Successive Scoutmasters during these years were Vic Crawford, Bernard Duchesne and Bill White. The Cubs were in the charge of Mrs Barbara Marriott, and she was succeeded as Akela by Mrs Doreen Cole.

The Colehill Guides have an unbroken history from their foundation in the 'twenties. "Jimmy" Hewett remained in charge after the war, before being succeeded by Irene Smart, and Mrs Ethel Orton, with the Melverley Guides, until its Company closed, in the 'sixties, then moved to the Colehill Company. Mrs Rideout was Captain of the Melverley Guides after the war, and Mrs Muriel Rowe was in charge of the Brownie Pack, which carried on longer than the Guides, in fact, until the closure of the School in 1969. As Muriel King, she had been a founder member of the Pack more than thirty years previously.

Scouts, Guides, Cubs and Brownies seem to have prospered over the years, benefitting from the vast influx of young families, as the population mushroomed.

A fund was started after the war by the "Welcome Home and War Memorial Committee", of which the indefatigable Reg Welch was secretary, to commemorate those who did not return. One worthy object suggested for disposing of the money donated was the provision of a *new* Parish Hall. There had, it may be remembered, been some dispute, much earlier, as to the ownership of the original Parish Hall, it being contended in some quarters that it belonged to the *village* rather than the Church. It seems likely that this dispute still rankled (as, indeed, it still does today with some of the older villagers) when the idea of a new hall was mooted. The suggested site, when the matter was being discussed back in 1947, was at the crossroads, on the corner diagonally opposite the Church. This was, of course, before the building of the council houses at Marshfield. After much more debate, and the lapse of more than twenty years, the Memorial Hall was eventually erected, near the old Village School.

A curious example of petty bureaucracy is recorded in the Middlehill School "log" in 1953, with an entry noting that the school had been advised by the Ordnance Survey that the districts known as Pilford and Middlehill would in future be termed "Colehill". The school was being modernised, in a modest sort of way, in these years following the war. Oil heaters were installed, to supplement the coal fire, in 1956. The old "tortoise" coke stove was still in use at this time. Central heating was installed in the following year.

In 1961, the playing field for the school was created on the site of one of the old gravel pits. The area of this has sadly diminished since then as the school expanded and additional classrooms were erected on the site across the road from the original buildings. A telephone was provided for the use of the headmistress in 1964, thus enabling her to deal with emergencies without the need of a tiresome, and time-consuming, walk to the Post Office. Miss Mildred Gillett was the Head at this time, having been appointed in 1955. She reigned for fourteen years, until her retirement, and presided over the vast expansion of the school during the 'sixties. The roll had almost trebled from the 150 pupils attending when she first came to the school. Looking back, in her retirement, she, herself a Dorset woman, has commented favourably upon the changes wrought upon the school, in an academic sense, by the newcomers, with their more sophisticated, urban backgrounds.

The School also housed the latest version of the County Library, in 1961, long before the building of separate premises nearby. This was open, during school term only, for half an hour at midday on Mondays. Colehill was gradually being provided with the amenities of modern life, although some districts had to wait longer for these than the area at the top of the hill.

In Leigh Lane, for example, electricity was not laid on until 1954 and gas was not available for another five or six years. Residents were still having to pump water from wells in their back gardens until the mains were laid in 1960, although the greater part of the village had had a mains supply for the previous fifty years. The supply of water was taken over by the Bournemouth and District Water Company, successor to the Bournemouth Gas and Water Company, which, in 1913, had absorbed the Wimborne Minster Water Works Co. Ltd. The water tower, giving the name to Tower Lane (or Turret Lane), erected in 1903, supplied the village by gravitational feed only at nighttime. However, even this once prominent landmark in the village, having served its purpose for eighty years, has become redundant and has been demolished. One house, at least, in Middlehill Road, continued to receive its water direct from a spring on the slopes of Cannon Hill for many years afterwards.

Street lighting, debated by the Parish Council for more than sixty years, eventually came to the village in the late 'fifties, with the building of a new road, Weston Road, where lamps were installed, lit by electricity. As other new roads spread over the heathland, so too did the street lighting. The older roads in the village remained unlit, apart from a solitary lamp at the Post Office crossroads, until 1963, when the Rural District Council, supported by the Parish Council, made itself responsible for street lighting in the built-up part of the village. The whole area, Wimborne included, lacked a sewerage system until early in the 'sixties. Earlier, when the first of the council houses at Marshfield were built, a small local sewage works was provided to serve them, behind a copse at the back of the houses. This small wood was part of an extensive plot of land purchased in 1958 by Lieutenant-Colonel P.G. Wavish from the Bankes Estate. His house, which had once been two Estate cottages, standing in Smugglers Lane, was included in the sale.

The scene was then set for the huge explosion of population. The small cul-de-sac, Whiteways, on part of the old Beaucroft Estate, was opened up for housing, taking its name from the builder of the properties, Albert White, in the late 'fifties. The first of the new large housing estates, built on the site of the old Leigh Vineries, followed. Earlier, Mackays had established a subsidiary, Stourbank Nurseries, at Little Canford; the Colehill business was sold to Cummings, who installed Lindsay Kerr as the resident manager. However, it failed to flourish and was closed down, and apart from one or two isolated individual businesses which survived for a year or two longer, the glasshouses were all demolished in the late 'fifties and early 'sixties. The new housing estate was followed by others which have since swallowed up much of the heathland, and agricultural land, too, in the eastern half of the village, on the old Uddens Estate.

Serious flooding affected Leigh Road, the main A31 road at that time, long before the building of the by-pass, near the Common, during the wet weather of 1961.

It seems ironical that, at the very moment when the village was set to expand on such a scale, with the prospect, given the provision of access to the railway by, perhaps, a "Halt" – the Southern Railway, before the war had been petitioned, unsuccessfully, for just such a station at Uddens – of considerably increasing the traffic on the line running below the hill, it was decided to close it. It had long since been reduced to the status of a country branch line. The summer timetable of 1955 shows that there were ten trains each weekday in each direction between Brockenhurst and Wimborne. It was possible to catch a train from Wimborne soon after seven in the morning and to be in London by ten. In addition, the line carried eight trains daily starting from Salisbury, with a corresponding return service. There was goods traffic, too, and on summer Saturdays, use was made of the line as a relief route for main line expresses, to avoid congestion at Bournemouth. The local service was reduced to a total of four trains in each direction on a Sunday. However, the railway succumbed, like many others, following the Beeching Report. The line closed to passenger traffic in 1964, and one track was removed, the other remaining for a few more years, to serve goods trains plying to and from the Army petroleum depot at West Moors.

The posts for the level crossing gates in Leigh Lane, redundant for so many years, were still standing in 1949, when Dennis Curran became the tenant of the old crossing-keeper's cottage, then still owned by what had become British Railways. The property was sold to the Currans in 1967. The track bed of the old line still remains, although sections of it have been sold off by the Dorset County Council, who inherited it, into private ownership.

As the houses and bungalows spread across Colehill, so too did the pine trees on Cannon Hill. The area to the north of the "spine" had been sold by the Uddens Estate some years earlier to the Forestry Commission, and the trees there were very well established. The more southerly part of the Hill was leased to the Commission for 199 years. The land was ploughed and left fallow in 1961 and 1962, at which time there was an unimpeded view over the Stour Valley to the south, along the entire length of the bridle track running along the "spine" – dubbed locally as "Cannon Hill Pier". A variety of trees were then planted – Scots Pine, Larch and Tsuga, the Hemlock Spruce.

Miss J.V. Moffat still ran her smallholding, keeping pigs and raising vegetables and soft fruit, for several more years, on the slope between the Hill and Middlehill Road. But that, too, disappeared many years ago, beneath a rash of new houses. This swallowed up yet more of the Uddens Estate, of which, following the sale of Pilford Farm, very little now remains on Colehill, apart from that part of Cannon Hill leased by the Forestry Commission.

The Parish Council has had to continue to defend the civil identity of the village, as in the inter-war years, against greedy neighbours. Bournemouth wanted to swallow the entire village in 1948. Five years later, the Wimborne Urban District Council was reviving its old claims, and trying to annex the parish.

And so Colehill thrives: Andrew Jones, Martin Neeves,

Joyce Plumb and Bernard Russell, among others who have endowed the village with their various talents, will be remembered by many in a more recent era. Much of the past is gone, and some, no doubt, is best forgotten. We would do well to cherish our not inconsiderable history, however, and it is to be hoped that this account will help to perpetuate it. It is certainly not a complete record: there are still mysteries to be unravelled, awaiting the attention of some future researcher.

A letter, beautifully written and most courteously worded, in rather quaint old-fashioned language, came into my hands some years ago. It was written by Major William J.E. Noble, grand-nephew of the celebrated Australian test cricketer, M.A. Noble, living at Highett, in the Australian State of Victoria. Addressed to "The Postmaster or Mistress, Cole Hill, or District environ, East Dorsetshire", it was an enquiry about a long-lost ancestor, living at Legan Lodge, Cole Hill, in 1836. John Dacombe passed the letter to me, thinking I might help. But that mystery remains unsolved. There is more research to be done, and more history to be written.

TOP OF ROWLANDS HILL, seen from the north-west in the 1950s, with Highland Road running off to the left. The railway line, curving into Wimborne, runs from left to right across the top of the picture.